The Most Powerful Wealth-Building Strategies Finally Revealed

WEALTHCLASSES PUBLISHING
www.WealthclassesPublishing.com

THE BANKER'S CODE
The Most Powerful Wealth-Building Strategies Finally Revealed
George Antone
www.TheBankersCodeBook.com

WEALTHCLASSES PUBLISHING
www.WealthClassesPublishing.com

FIRST EDITION

Printed in the United States of America.

Book design by TLC Graphics, *www.TLCGraphics.com*
Cover by Monica Thomas / Interior by Erin Stark
Cover photo: ©*iStockphoto.com/JLGutierrez*

Events in the book have been fictionalized for educational content and impact.

ISBN-10: 0982704518
ISBN-13: 978-0-9827045-1-6

This publication is designed to provide information with regard to the subject matter covered. It is sold with the understanding that the publisher and author are not engaged in rendering real estate, legal, accounting, tax, or other professional services and that the publisher and author are not offering such advice in this publication. If real estate, legal, or other expert assistance is required, the services of a competent professional person should be sought. The publisher and author specifically disclaim any liability that is incurred from the use or application of the contents of this book.

I DEDICATE THIS BOOK TO:

Paul,
France,
Jacqueline,
Gisele,
Michel,
and Pierre.
You helped shape my life.
And to the many students we have come across.

TABLE OF CONTENTS

FOREWORD

ANTHONY ROBBINS SAID IT BEST: "IT IS IN YOUR MOMENTS OF DECISION that your destiny is shaped." I believe that. I believe that the decisions we make define the trajectory of our lives and, ultimately, our fortune.

I made one of those decisions when I began my own wealth-building journey as a struggling landscaper, living in a one-room apartment. In a little more than three years (and without any real estate investing experience) I could have retired after building a successful 400-plus-unit portfolio. I now have more than 7,000 multi-units that provided more passive income every month than most people make in a year! And I've raised more than $65M in private money in less than six years. I can say with confidence that I know more than a thing or two about building wealth.

And when people ask me what the secret to success is, I simply tell them: Begin with the decision to change.

I've been challenged a lot about what I teach, and I was genuinely surprised to find my own mindset challenged with this book. What a treat it was to read a book from cover to cover and still want more.

I've known George Antone for several years now. It's rare to find a brilliant financier mind that can also share sophisticated information in such a simple way. I know that, like me, you'll immediately find yourself-absorbing sophisticated wealth-building strategies easily and quickly. You'll enthusiastically explore new paradigms, uncovering amazing, new possibilities for building wealth. His simple, down-to-earth style takes complex techniques and, with George's unique touch, breaks it all down into a step-by-step approach that anyone can understand and, more important, implement.

But be warned – *The Banker's Code* is truly for individuals interested in taking their wealth to a whole new level. It's not a book that just talks about what could be. This book will change the way you look at the core of your financial life and will have your mind reeling with amazing possibilities that can help you create the life that dreams are made of.

As George shares in the book, investors and private lenders need each other. This book opens your eyes to a business model that has been around for a very long time – being the banker without using your money. Just like the banks do it.

Today's economic woes may be dominating many conversations, but George's book comes at a perfect time. I'm betting that almost every reader will be wishing they'd had this information a long time ago. *The Banker's Code* is a game changer and can be the difference between struggling with your wealth building – or not!

Many years ago, I made the decision to change my destiny. George made the decision to change his destiny. You now have in your hands a book that can change your destiny. Once again, "It is in your moments of decision that your destiny is shaped." Make that decision to read this book cover to cover. Get ready to be blown away!

DAVID LINDAHL
Founder, Creative Success Alliance

ACKNOWLEDGEMENTS

WRITING MY FIRST BOOK, *THE WEALTHY CODE,* CHANGED MY LIFE. I have since realized that I really enjoy sharing the wealth of information I've learned.

Writing this second book, *The Banker's Code,* was an easier task because of the support of many people. Everyone at WealthClasses.com has helped me in a number of different ways, especially Stephanie May, who helped in many ways write this book. Also, thanks to my business partners, Gary Boomershine, Haider Nazar, and Phong Dang. Willie Hooks, you are a true inspiration to me and to others. Coaches Mary, Ray, and Marc, thank you for always being there and supporting me in times of need. Julia Jordan, I have no words to describe how amazing you are! Thanks for always being you. Swanee Heidberg, thank you for allowing me to hassle you with this book. You are a great friend. And to all of our students that have taken this information and implemented it, changing your lives with it – Thank You! It's *you* that keep us going and *you* that help us achieve our goal: To end financial suffering and help people get the wealth they need to live the lifestyle they desire. It's *you* we celebrate.

Nor would this book have been possible without Tom and Tamara Dever and everyone else at TLC Graphics. Thank you so much.

THE INSPIRATION FOR THIS BOOK

The Secret to the Greatest Dynasty the World Has Ever Known . . .

Long ago, in the 1700s, lived a man named Mayer,
born in poverty in the ghettos of Frankfurt.

One day, he discovered a secret — a great secret
powerful enough to make him fabulously wealthy.

Mayer taught his five sons this secret
and then sent them to live throughout Europe.

They, in turn, used the secret to build the greatest
international financial dynasty the world has ever known.

Today, this family continues to pass its secret from
one generation to the next, and the family's influence
and power have reached every corner of the earth.

They are…the Rothschilds.

The Banker's Code was inspired by this true story.

Get ready to learn the bankers' secrets!

CHAPTER ONE

...And Then There Was Banking!

I WALKED INTO MY MENTOR'S OFFICE, LOADED WITH QUESTIONS.

"Let me ask you this. What's the most powerful, wealth-building strategy ever known to man?" I asked.

My mentor, a successful, down-to-earth, approachable man, had built his wealth in real estate. I had met him only a few years earlier, and he had already changed my life with his wisdom.

"Hello to you, too," he chuckled, pointing to a chair.

"Sorry! Hello!" I replied with a sheepish grin as I settled into the chair.

"So, you want to learn about the most powerful wealth-building strategies known to man?"

"Yep! I'm curious what you think they are. The information you shared with me a few weeks ago about passive income was powerful, but I want to know what you think stands out from all the other strategies you and I have talked about."

A few weeks earlier we had discussed the code the wealthy use in generating great cash flow from their investments.

"The absolute, most powerful wealth strategy ever known to man? I can tell you with certainty what it is," my mentor announced with confidence.

1

"It's not something I think I know, it's something I know I know! And the richest people in the world will tell you the same thing. However, the majority of the population doesn't know what it is."

He eyed me carefully, drawing out his words as he continued. "I'm not sure you're ready for it, though. It's not that it's difficult. In fact, it's quite simple, but that's also its danger. It gives you power…but most people can't handle that power," he said mysteriously.

Was he talking about wealth building or something else? I wasn't sure.

"Come on, man!" I chuckled.

After a few minutes of listening to me beg while he checked his e-mail, he swung his chair towards me and replied, "Okay, after I whet your appetite, I'm going to send you to a friend of mine. Once you speak to him, come back to me, and you'll know the secret. You'll know the most powerful wealth-building strategy known to man!"

Have you ever wondered if there's a secret so great that it can help you live a much better life financially?

There is, and this information has built dynasties.

Let's start from the beginning.

Who taught you about becoming wealthy? Parents? Teachers? Friends? Priests? And where are they financially? The saying goes that if you want to be a billionaire, learn from a billionaire. If you want to be a millionaire, learn from a millionaire. If you want to be broke, learn from someone who's broke. Most people are learning about money and about being rich from the wrong people.

The people who know about the "secret" strategies described in this book have kept this knowledge to themselves, selfishly passing it from generation to generation. Consider the Rothschilds, the greatest banking dynasty the world has ever known, still going strong, still passing these same strategies from one generation to the next.

And yet, this secret has been "hidden" right in front of us the entire time. It's been available to practically everyone. It can be found on nearly every corner of this country.

Here's my promise. I will reveal to you, in the pages of this book, the most powerful wealth strategy known to man. What's in this book will almost certainly challenge your beliefs about money. All I ask is that you keep an open mind while you read, and you will learn some amazing things.

The Secret Lies in the Game of *Monopoly*

Many people have played the classic board game *Monopoly*. As children, we grew up playing the game with friends and family, yet most of us never noticed the secret that in real life has created billionaires. This secret allows you to win *Monopoly* every single time. What is that secret?

Take a moment to think about it.

Buying four green homes and a hotel? Nope. There's no guarantee you'll win the game with that.

Buying Park Place and Mayfair? Nope. There's no guarantee you'll win the game with that, either.

In fact, the secret to winning the game is to be the banker.

Think about it. The banker wins every single time.

Why is that?

It's because the game players are playing with one set of rules – the investor's rules. The banker is playing with a different set of rules – the banker's rules. So, there are really two games going on. The banker's rules are all about making the most money with the least risk. The investor's rules are about making the most money, but investors incur more risk than do the bankers.

In the board game, one player (investor) wins while all the other players (also investors) lose. However, the banker always wins. Obviously, real life is different. Many investors do "win," but many also lose. In fact, a lot more investors lose the game because they're playing with investor's rules, rules stacked to the banker's advantage. Keep reading to find out why.

The second game in *Monopoly* is the banker's game. The bankers follow the banker's rules. The banker's rules are very different from the investor's rules – they were written by bankers *for* bankers. And here's the rub. The investor's rules were written by the bankers as well! So, which rules do you think are more favorable to the banks? The bankers have written both sets of rules to work for them!

> **Investors and bankers play two different games with two sets of rules. However, the bankers wrote the rules for both games. Whom do you think the rules favor?**

The banker plays a safer game and makes more money. If he needs money, he can create more money. We'll cover the banker's rules later, but it's important to understand that the rules of both games were written by bankers.

So, the first step to making money – like the bank – is to adopt the mindset of the banker and play by the banker's rules.

> **The secret is to learn to be the bank – adopt the mindset of the banker and play by the banker's rules.**

The Proof

The average person is playing in a game they don't even know exists. Sadly, they're losing that game, too. This reminds me of the science fiction movie, *The Matrix*, where the main character in the movie, Neo, is introduced to "...the truth about his world by shedding light on the dark secrets that have troubled him for so long: 'You've felt it your entire life, that there's something wrong with the world. You don't know what it is, but it's there, like a splinter in your mind, driving you mad.' Ultimately, Morpheus illustrates to Neo what the Matrix is – a reality beyond reality that controls all of their lives, in a way that Neo can barely comprehend."

When it comes to our world, we're also involved in a game that we have no idea exists. Unfortunately, the reward for that game is our money. The other team is beating us at this game, and we're constantly having to fork over money. This game is called "the financing game," and our opponents are the financial institutions. In fact, we actually have two opponents: the financial institutions and the government.

Let's look at the proof.

Of the average American's income, 34.5% goes towards paying interest alone. That doesn't include principal – just interest. Interest on credit cards, mortgages, car loans, furniture, among other things. The recipients of that interest are the financial institutions.

Another 30% of the average American's income goes towards paying income taxes. The recipient of that revenue is the government.

And finally, less than 5% of the average American's income goes towards savings.

Consider those numbers. 64.5% of the average American's income is going to financial institutions and the government. That means we're spending two-thirds of our time working to pay the financial institutions and the government. Put differently, the average American works from January 1st all the way through August 31st for financial institutions and the government. Then, we live on the money we have earned from September 1st to December 31st. Or so we think – until we realize that it's actually worse – a lot worse.

In *The Matrix,* Neo discovers that the world he knew is not what he thinks; it's actually being controlled, and everyone is basically a puppet.

Unfortunately, in real life so are we.

The proof is in the numbers. As noted above, the average American has become a slave to the financial system. And for those of you who are "debt free" and pay off your credit cards every month, you have a lot to learn, as well. We've been conditioned to work hard while helping the bankers become rich.

But this book is about to change that for you. You are about to become "the banker."

A Basic Look at How Banks Work

We've been conditioned to deposit our money into banks, "saving" money in our savings account (or checking, money market, CDs, etc.). We're trained to think that our money is safe in those bank accounts, because we trust the bankers.

We're then paid a measly interest rate, and just in case that measly rate wasn't a slap in the face, we have to pay taxes on it to the government. The bank then uses our money to leverage up to 10 times (or more, in certain cases) by using the fractional reserve system. Our $1,000 deposit generates up to $10,000 in loans for the bank!

We then proceed to borrow that money from the bank (our own money) at a much higher interest rate, and they tie up our homes and other collateral, just in case we default. So, because we're borrowing money from the banks, they now can set their own terms: the interest rate, the collateral requirement, the term of the loan, etc.

We complain that the terms of the loan don't favor us, but then we're reminded of The Golden Rule: "He who has the gold makes the rules." Banks make the rules. The extremely wealthy make the rules. No getting around it.

So, we sign on the dotted line and borrow the money (remember, it was *our* money) on their terms.

If we should default, they end up taking all the collateral they tied up. That's when we realize they tied up a *lot* more collateral than what we borrowed. We are reminded again that they set the rules – so we have to play by their terms. They "dump" our collateral for nothing, just to get their money back. And they do get their money back. We took on a lot more risk than we needed, but we had no choice. The bankers set the rules.

But most of us don't default. As we pay the loan, they re-lend us the same money, again and again. They're moving money fast! They're taking little risk and making a lot of money. We realize we're still paying interest long after we've paid the bank the original loan amount. Moreover, they've generated many more loans from the same money we paid them, and we're still paying them. We feel like we have no choice! But we do.

We can get angry at the bank and play the victim. Or, we can become the banker.

We're conditioned to deposit money into banks. Why not deposit it in our own personal "bank"? Why not lend our own money to others, taking on the safer position and making more money? Why not leverage our own money up to 10 times and lend it out?

You can do all of this – and make a lot of money!

But before you start counting your billions, you need to understand something about this book. It was not my intent to provide for you a "how-to-do-it" shortcut to wealth; rather, my primary goal in writing this book was to get you to open your eyes to the possibilities, to recognize opportunities, to help you to see what's right in front of you.

With that understanding, let's jump into building the foundation to being your own banker.

Being a banker is all about adopting their mindset and their rules; understanding how they manage money and how they use financial strategies to make a lot more money; and ultimately, working to leave a legacy to the next generation of bankers in your family.

"Is this for real?" I asked. "Is it really *possible for just anyone to be a banker?"*

"We're not talking about opening a real bank, George. We're not talking about getting a banking license. But we are *talking about making money just like a bank," my mentor patiently replied.*

"If you adopt the mindset, the rules, and the strategies of a banker," he added, "you can have a much better life financially. Just don't let the power get to you. Always follow the banker's rules."

"And don't forget…bankers make more money than investors, with a lot less risk."

CHAPTER SUMMARY

- Investors play by the banker's rules. The bankers play by their own rules.
- The investor's rules are stacked to the banker's advantage.
- Of the average American's income, 34.5% goes towards paying interest alone; 30% goes towards taxes. That's an indication that the average American is working two-thirds of his time for bankers and the government.
- This book's primary objective is to open your eyes to the possibilities.

CHAPTER TWO

It's Nothing But A Financing Game

"IN FACT, LET ME SHARE ONE THING WITH YOU RIGHT NOW, GEORGE. THIS 15-minute lesson will be an awakening for you," he predicted confidently.

"Grab a pen and paper. This – the first secret about banking – you do not want to miss. So get ready to write; let's dive in."

I grabbed a clean sheet of paper.

It's About Cash Flow First

Why do people invest?

For one of two reasons: cash flow or capital gains.

The wealthy recognize (as I explained in *The Wealthy Code*) that they need cash flow to pay for their living expenses and lifestyle. They also recognize that investments for capital gains are nothing more than money that will buy more income-producing assets in the future.

But the middle class and poor tend to invest for capital gains only. For example, investments, such as buying stocks for the long term ("buy and hold" strategy), are very typical. The general public has been conditioned by the financial institutions to think like that. We'll cover this later in the book.

Bankers – and other wealthy people – realize that it's about cash flow first.

So How Do You Generate Cash Flow?

Cash flow is about arbitrage (creating a spread between the cost of borrowed money and what an investment pays). Arbitrage is nothing more than a leveraged strategy.

The figure below illustrates that.

FIGURE 1: Breaking "wealth" into basic components

To create an arbitrage opportunity, you need to have the following criteria (a simplified formula for passive income) in place:

1. An income-producing asset (such as an apartment building, rental property, insurance policy, business, bonds)
2. A lender that is willing to lend against the asset as collateral (obtain leverage)
3. Income that is larger than the loan payments and expenses related to the asset

That's it! That's the simple formula for passive income. Some individuals can buy an asset for all cash without leverage, but for most people cash is a limited resource. Adding the second step allows you to scale up your passive income.

An investor buying an apartment building can use the apartment building as collateral for the loan. The investor puts some money down, borrows the rest from the bank, and creates the arbitrage. This meets all three of the criteria above.

Similarly, an investor buying a small rental property can use the property as collateral for the loan. The rent is the income. The investor puts some money down, borrows the rest from the bank, and creates the arbitrage. This also meets all three of the criteria above.

For a business owner buying, let's say, a car wash, the business is the income-producing asset (criterion no. 1); and lenders are willing to lend against it to help the business owner buy it (criterion no. 2); and finally, hopefully, the income is larger than the loan payments and the expenses of the business (criterion no. 3).

Obviously, the business owner has to deal with the headaches of running the business, potential lawsuits, employees, and other day-to-day issues. Similarly, the landlord in the previous examples has to deal with the headaches of tenants and toilets.

Let's suppose you could buy a black box from a retail store and place it on your shelf at home. Let's also suppose that the black box generates $1,000 per month in income for you. That allows you to meet criterion no. 1 in our formula. Suppose that a lender is willing to lend you the money to buy it (for example, the retail store offers financing to buy it). This allows you to meet criterion no. 2. Now suppose the loan payments are $700 per month. This allows you to keep a difference (passive income) of $300 per month (remember, the black box is generating $1,000 per month). This allows you to meet criterion no. 3. The black box is headache-free with no hassles. It just sits on your shelf at home and makes you money.

Now, if you could buy as many of these black boxes as you want, would you prefer to own the car wash, rental properties, or this black box? Obviously, the black box.

The point of this is to illustrate that the main reason we buy some of these assets for passive income (the car wash, Laundromats, rental properties, self storage) is for the sake of generating passive income first. We don't buy them simply for the sake of buying them or owning them. In fact, when I hear people say how excited they are to own real estate, I realize they don't own enough real estate to know what they're talking about. We own real estate or these businesses for the sake of passive income first.

Now, the black box doesn't really exist, but the question is, what is the closest thing to this black box? Well, the answer may surprise you.

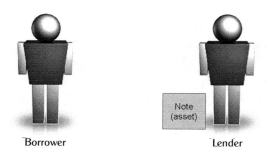

Borrower   Lender

FIGURE 2: Borrower signs a promissory note to lender, which becomes an asset to the lender

Suppose a borrower borrows $50,000 at 10% from a lender and signs a mortgage to the lender. The lender now has an income-producing asset (the piece of paper – the mortgage – is now an asset that produces an income – the interest – for them). This meets criterion no. 1 in our simple, passive-income formula.

Now the lender can borrow against this asset (the mortgage) at a lower rate. This is called "hypothecation." In our example, the lender pledges this mortgage as collateral for a loan of $50,000 at, say, 7%. This meets criterion no. 2.

At this point, the lender receives payments at 10% interest and pays 7% interest, leaving a 3% spread. This meets criterion no. 3.

Let's step back for a second and think about what just happened. To generate passive income, you need, at the core of it, two things: an asset and leverage (borrowed money). You use the asset to pledge as collateral to get the borrowed money. Most people have to find a physical structure or a business (as the asset) to pledge as collateral to borrow that money. But the banker simply *prints* the collateral, the mortgage document, and as long as someone is willing to sign it, that document is now an income-producing asset that can generate passive income!

Investors have to buy physical structures, such as properties or businesses, to use as collateral to get leverage (borrowed money) so they can generate cash flow. Then they are forced to deal with the aggravations of these assets, such as tenant problems, overflowing toilets, employee hassles, inevitable lawsuits, and a myriad of other nightmare scenarios.

Bankers simply print a piece of paper – a mortgage – and as long as someone is willing to sign it as a borrower, it serves as the collateral for borrowed money. This is known as hypothecation. The end result is the same. Cash flow.

So, a banker with a filing cabinet of 40 mortgages, each generating $300 per month, is the equivalent to a landlord with a lot of homes, each generating $300 per month. So, what is the closest thing to that black box? The banker's mortgages.

Bankers create collateral out of paper, borrow against it, and create an arbitrage opportunity immediately. This is power! But, it gets better.

Other investors, as you will find out in upcoming chapters, take on a bigger risk than the lender. They also play by the lender's rules.

You create your own arbitrage opportunity as a lender by creating collateral out of thin air, shifting the risk to the borrower (putting you in a safer position), generating the cash flow you're looking for, and writing the rules by which the borrower has to play.

You accomplished the same thing as investors (i.e., arbitrage), but *much* more easily with a lot *less* hassle!

It's a Financing Game!

Bankers recognize that generating cash flow from spreads is nothing more than a financing game. Most real estate investors think it's about real estate. It's not. It's a financing game for them, as well. The only reason they purchase a building is for the sake of creating a spread. It's *not* about the tenants. It's *not* about the physical property. A building is simply collateral that the bank is willing to lend against so that the investor can make a spread.

Similarly, a business owner buying a business (for example, a Laundromat) for some cash flow thinks it's about the Laundromat. It's not. He buys it simply to generate a spread. He uses the business as collateral for a loan to create a spread. In reality, it's a financing game.

Bankers recognize that, and they play it quite well. They create the collateral from a piece of paper, creating spreads from that all day long. They know they're in the business of financing, safety, and making lots of money. They have the best position.

Let Them Think What They Want. We Know the Truth.

Bankers know it. They've shifted the risk to the borrower. They're in position to make money, and they tied up the borrower's collateral, just in case. They're in the business of financing and safety.

But they need borrowers. They need to use other people's money to create spreads.

So they condition the population to borrow money using good collateral and the banker's rules. They've shifted the risk to the borrowers (as we shall find out). They've conditioned everyone to invest for capital gains. This allows the invested money to sit with the bankers and make even more money, because the money is "dead." It's not moving for the rest of us.

They condition the population about "saving" their money in their banks, becoming a chunk of their money source they can then use in creating spreads.

They know they have the most powerful wealth-building strategies ever known to man. But they keep it a secret – otherwise we all become bankers and no one is left to be a borrower!

Welcome to banking.

I arrived in San Ramon, found the park my mentor had told me about, parked my car, and walked across the open field he mentioned.

I noticed Dr. Jazz right away, sitting on the park bench at the top of the hill, with a commanding view of the San Ramon Valley. The sun, hidden from view for the past several days, was shining now, and Dr. Jazz was soaking it in as if he were relaxing on a Caribbean beach instead of a park bench in California.

I approached him hesitantly, nervous about meeting him. He was a fastidious man with piercing eyes, eyes that radiated intelligence. In his brown suit, he looked older than I thought (in his 70s I decided). When he spoke, his voice calmed me instantly.

"So, your mentor tells me you're a pretty sharp man. He tells me he's very proud of what you have accomplished . . . so far," he chuckled. "He asked me to tell you a story, a story that I've told to only a few very close friends. And it is because of your mentor that I have agreed to do so."

I think I mumbled, "Wow, thank you."

After some small talk, he asked, "Have you ever been to New Jersey? No? Well, the view from this spot reminds me of the Princeton campus there. I spent many, many hours there with my own mentor, a friend I think you will be interested in hearing more about. He was a remarkable man, and he talked to me about things that he did not talk to most people about.

"He was a genius with numbers, an intellectual who understood finance at its core and who was able to see things with numbers that most people could not."

I was getting interested now and beginning to see why my mentor wanted me to meet Dr. Jazz.

"He was your mentor?" I asked.

"Yes. In fact, he was — and still is — considered one of the greatest scientific minds of the 20th century. I cannot reveal his name at this time, but let's call him Herbert," said Dr. Jazz. "And yes, he was my mentor and my friend, and he changed my life."

"Scientific mind? You mean he was a scientist?" I asked incredulously. "I know scientists discover or invent all kinds of . . . stuff," I stammered, "but how did he help you? I mean, how did he help you become so . . ."

"Wealthy?" Dr. Jazz laughed. He got up to stretch, and said, "Young man, let's walk a bit and keep things moving." As we slowly walked around the park, he began to tell me a story.

"Herbert was a genius with numbers, and he could strategize a hundred different ways to reach a goal without even thinking about it. Most people don't know he was fascinated with finance, and in fact, he wrote about it quite a bit, most of it in his private manuscripts."

Dr. Jazz told me about how he had met Herbert at Princeton while working on campus, about how the two had formed an unlikely friendship, and how Herbert had tutored and mentored him until his death. He told me more about Herbert's writings and how he would draw pictures, notes, and ideas all over the margins of his books and notebooks.

"My friend," Dr. Jazz finally said, "the sun has long since left us, and I'm afraid I must leave, too. But if you would like, we can continue tomorrow, right here in this beautiful spot."

The next day, I could hardly wait, and I smiled to myself as I realized I was an hour early this time. I had armed myself with my own list of questions, notes, and drawings I wanted to discuss with this wonderful man.

"Ah, I see you came prepared and eager to know more. That's good! Let's take a walk." We strolled around the park some more, and he paused now and again to push a stone or a small branch to the side of the walkway gingerly and efficiently with the tip of his shoe.

"Tell me more about Herbert, and why finance?" I blurted out.

By the time we took a small detour to a nearby café, I felt like I had known this man for a long time. He reminded me of my grandfather. Once he had doctored his coffee to his liking, he said, "Herbert was fascinated by numbers, not for the sake of making money in finance, but for the sake of challenging himself with discovering something new. He believed that there is something about finance that could result in wealth while minimizing risk, and he ultimately discovered the ideal way of doing that.

"Herbert wrote one special book, a manuscript really, that contains those financial secrets I'm sharing with you," he said. "He taught me what was in it. Fascinating information. Beautiful stuff, George. Then, at his death, his will stipulated that six copies be made of his original manuscript and that they — including the original manuscript — be distributed to seven different people. I received one; his family received one; a young, homeless boy received one; and I am not sure where the others ended up. I have been the caretaker of mine for many years, telling only a very few about it. This manuscript contains some of the most amazing, fantastic secrets that have given me, and some of the most powerful people in history, our wealth."

I was getting more and more excited by the minute.

After several hours of chatting about the fascinating experiences of his younger years, Dr. Jazz looked at his watch and sighed, "I'm afraid I must go now," he said. "Let's meet again tomorrow; I'll bring you a surprise."

CHAPTER SUMMARY

- Generating cash flow boils down to following a specific "formula," outlined in *The Wealthy Code*.
- At a basic level, generating cash flow requires two things: an income-producing asset and the leverage (borrowed money) to buy this asset.
- For business owners and investors, the income-producing asset typically turns out to be a physical structure with many aggravations. For bankers, the income-producing asset becomes a piece of paper they print and the borrower signs.
- Business owners or investors think they are in the business of doing what the structures they bought do, but the reality is, they are in the business of generating a spread in the business of financing.
- That's what the banker recognizes.
- For more information and additional training about arbitrage, please refer to the Resources page in the back of the book.

CHAPTER THREE

Pick a Team First

"YES, IT'S THE MANUSCRIPT," DR. JAZZ LAUGHED. "HERE IS HERBERT'S work. Look. See for yourself. Are your hands clean?" he chided.

I could see why. The manuscript was very heavy; thick and covered with leather, darkened now by time and countless handlings with a thick, braided cord, shiny from wear, tied around its middle. The pages were of heavy paper, yellowed, of course, with age, and every page was covered with writings, graphs, and drawings. But I was more fascinated with the countless abbreviations, notes, and pictures drawn everywhere in the margins. The title was etched on the cover: The Book of the Banker's Code.

In some cases, Herbert had apparently used his own shorthand, but it all looked like hieroglyphics to me. I hoped Dr. Jazz could read it all, and more important, that he would tell me everything!

"Are you ready to find out what some of this means?" he chuckled.

Dr. Jazz turned the pages of the manuscript gingerly and pointed to a diagram with three circles. A lot of arrows pointed back and forth between the circles, which simply said "Consumer," "Producer," and "Banker," with countless scribbles surrounding the circles.

"You need to start by trying to understand the teams in the game of finance. They boil down to three. Understanding the mindsets and the role of each team is critical to your success in finance," Dr. Jazz began.

"The better you understand the teams, the more evident it becomes which one will always win. In fact, it's almost not fair how much easier one of those teams has it. You will soon understand why this team doesn't want many people joining them," he continued.

Pick Your Team

The world is divided into three teams: consumers, producers, and bankers.

Consumers use products and services. They are the ones who buy the latest electronics, smart phones, and impressive cars.

Producers provide products and services. They're the ones that manufacturer and/or sell the latest gizmos: phones, cars, televisions, food, and more. Everything a consumer uses comes from a producer. The producers are the ones that create jobs and hire consumers to work for them. They are masters of systems that generate profits. Many believe this is the most interesting position to be in because it is always challenging and, with the right mindset, can be seen as a game for adults.

> ## The world is divided into three teams: consumers, producers, and bankers.

Bankers finance both consumers and producers. The consumer uses that money to buy products and services from the producer, and the producer uses that borrowed money to produce those products and services for the consumer. The bankers don't have to laugh all the way to the bank. After all, they own the bank, so they laugh while sitting in the bank! They are masters of *shifting risk* to the borrower and *financing*.

Every person has the option of choosing which side to play on. But most people think they are limited to being a consumer for the rest of their lives.

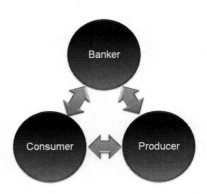

FIGURE 3: The three possible teams one can be on

Consumers have to work hard all their lives to pay for the financing of goods and services. They make up the majority of the world, and without them, producers and bankers would suffer. So it's in everyone's best interest to have consumers working hard in jobs and using borrowed money to buy goods and services. They aren't aware that they are always being conditioned to buy stuff or being persuaded into buying certain brands. They aren't aware of how producers and bankers team up to influence them into buying. Producers partner with advertising agencies, credit card companies (bankers), and the media to condition the consumer to spend borrowed money on "stuff." Hundreds of millions of dollars are spent on conditioning the consumer to spend money. The biggest companies in the world partner with experts to ensure that consumers spend.

This is not necessarily a bad thing. The consumer is buying something of value: a home, a car, a smart phone, food, and the like.

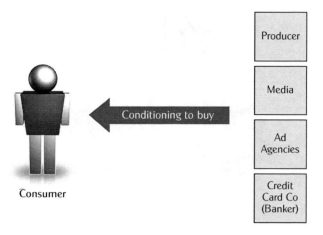

FIGURE 4: Consumers are being conditioned to buy

Producers borrow money from bankers, use that to generate products and services, and pass on the cost – along with hefty profits – of the borrowed money to the consumer. They focus on creating value to the consumers. Whether it's opening a restaurant, a nearby mall, a movie theater, or housing, producers are always looking at the needs and wants of consumers and providing stuff to satisfy those needs and wants. Producers have to focus on their systems generating a profit with the borrowed money; otherwise, it all backfires. Using borrowed money can turn around and hurt producers if they fail to turn a profit. Many entrepreneurs go out of business within a few years because they lack the skills needed to build a business.

Bankers, on the other hand, make the most money. They use borrowed money to lend out and tie up the borrowers' collateral. They cover their downside and let the upside take care of itself. They are masters of shifting risk to the borrowers. If borrowers fail to pay, they lose all the collateral to the bankers. The bank ties up enough collateral to make sure they make enough money. However, if the borrower is successful in paying back the banker, the banker makes money.

Either way, the banker wins. The *best* part of being the banker is that they recognize they don't need to have money to lend out. Through a combination of using borrowed money and "printing" money, they can make money, and lots of it. I'll explain this later.

Every person on this planet fits into at least one of these three teams (producers and bankers are, of course, also consumers). There is no other choice. By default, people start as consumers, but producers and bankers become the rich.

Every Producer Needs a Money Person

Consider the diagram below. The producers on the left-hand side – e.g. property rehabbers, property flippers, business owners, restaurant owners, Internet companies – all need money. All of them need to work with the banker (or money person) on the right-hand side. Producers need to first learn everything they can about the "job" on the left-hand side, including skills required. For example, as a property rehabber a producer needs to build a team of contractors and learn how to manage such teams, learn about the real estate business (estimating, making low offers on properties, selling properties fast once they are fixed up), and many other things. In addition to all that, they need to learn how to raise money to get all of it done.

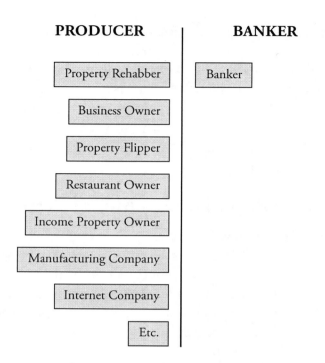

FIGURE 5: Producers need bankers. Bankers are in the money business

The banker (the money person) on the right just needs to learn how to borrow money to lend out and how to make their position safer by shifting the risk to the borrower. The banker can work with all these producers without having to learn much about their skills. And the banker just happens to be the most powerful position in the equation. The producer does all the work, takes all the risk, and gets paid last. The banker does the least amount of work, takes on the safer position, gets paid first, and makes more money.

Both the producer and the consumer think the banker needs to have his own money, and lots of it, to make money. Nothing could be further from the truth. And that's exactly why the banker wants to keep it a secret.

For Example

A producer decides to provide a product for consumers. The producer goes to the bank and gets a loan of $100,000 at 10% interest annually. In the process, the banker ties up enough collateral from the producer to cover the payment. By doing so, the banker has covered his downside.

The producer uses that money to hire experts (creating jobs), manufactures the product (more jobs created), and sells it to consumers through retail stores. The producer calculates that a retail price of $5 per unit will cover the cost of the interest to the bank, the cost of manufacturing, cost of goods, and other expenses, and provide a nice profit. He has just over 200,000 units to sell.

The consumer buys the product for $5, and that helps fulfill a need or want in their lives. It has value to them. The consumer uses their credit card to buy that $5 product. That ends up costing this consumer $5.12 (including interest).

The banker gets their $100,00 back, with interest from the producer, and makes an additional profit by lending money to consumers who use it to buy the product!

The producer passed on the cost of interest (including a profit) to the consumer.

So, finally, the consumer paid the credit card company (banker) some interest to buy the product, the producer the interest they paid the banker, and the producer their deserved profit.

The Consumer is Blinded

What's interesting about these three positions is the mindset of each. They all think their position is the right one. Very few look at the other, wishing they were in the other's position.

The consumer thinks the following:
- I don't like taking risks.
- Having a business (being a producer) is too risky.

- I'll save money to become wealthy (taking perhaps 40 or more years).

The producer thinks the following:
- I can't imagine working for someone else; I can never be a consumer.
- Having a job (being a consumer) is too risky.
- I can become rich in 10 years or less.

The banker thinks the following:
- I can't imagine having a job (consumer) or dealing with employees (producer).
- I make money off of money.
- I make money by following a very simple model and keeping my mouth shut about how simple it is.

The producer and banker understand that without the consumer, they can never make it. So they have to keep conditioning the consumer to spend money.

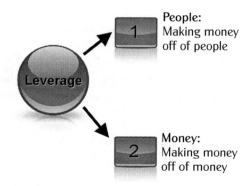

FIGURE 6: Producers and bankers using different types of leverage

The producer and banker also understand it's a game of leverage. However, the producer sees it as leveraging other people. By hiring people and having them follow a system, the producer makes money off of them. For example, he might pay someone $10 an hour and make $60 an hour off that person. The producer's leverage is about making money off of people. For example, Microsoft Corp. makes money from its thousands of employees. It might cost them a million dollars to finance and support a certain department over the period of a year, but the company might make four million dollars a year because of that department.

> ## The producer's leverage is mainly making money off of people.

The banker, on the other hand, sees it as making money off of money. To the banker, every dollar bill is equivalent to an employee. They can make money off that dollar bill. The banker looks at the dollar bill as an employee who doesn't sue them, doesn't take time off, ask for a raise, take sick days. So they might make 12 cents for every dollar they have. They prefer it that way, because making money off of money is a lot easier than having to deal with employees, scheduling headaches, and more. The dollar bill never complains.

Consider fund managers – mutual or hedge fund managers, for instance. They retain a few people to manage millions of dollars. Fund managers are considered bankers as well. This is an example of financial leverage. They make money off of money. The highest-paid hedge fund managers have gotten paid more than a billion dollars over the past few years!

> ## The banker's leverage is mainly making money off of money (financial leverage).

"Once you are very clear on how each player thinks and the value they bring to the game, it all starts making sense," Dr. Jazz said as he carefully turned the page.

I was amazed at the patience and generosity of this man. Our friendship was growing stronger every day, and I had so much to ask him, so much to learn from him. I prayed he would never stop sharing this information with me.

Then I realized my mind had strayed, and I quickly brought it back!

"It's not to say that one is any better than the other," offered Dr. Jazz. "There are reasons why and times when it's good to be in any of those positions. But understanding these teams is just the first step. Picking a team is the second. Then, getting educated on how to play on that team is the third step. Now, let's look at something more interesting," he suggested as he pointed to another remarkable, stick-figure diagram.

I grinned, and leaned forward so I could see better.

CHAPTER SUMMARY

- The world is divided into three teams: consumers, producers, and bankers.
- The consumer is conditioned to spend.
- The banker finances the producer and the consumer.
- Producers leverage people's time, skills, and efforts to make money.
- Producers (business owners and investors) need bankers.
- Bankers leverage money to make more money.

CHAPTER FOUR

Money, Interest, And Being A Private Lender

DR. JAZZ POINTED TO A DIAGRAM MADE UP OF TWO STICK FIGURES AND *paused for an uncomfortably long time. I could tell he was struggling to tell me something.*

"I'm not sure how to share this information," Dr. Jazz said, reluctantly. "It might sound bad, but it's not necessarily so. I'm not sure if you really need to know this, but…hmmm," he muttered without finishing the thought.

I couldn't figure out what he was about to say, but I kept thinking. After all, he was pointing at stick figures! *How bad could it be?*

Well, turns out it was certainly eye-opening!

Imagine a world with two people, Bob and Carl.

Bob has $1,000, and that represents all the money in their world.

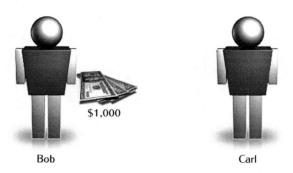

FIGURE 7: Bob and Carl with $1000 representing all the money in their world

Now, Carl needs $500, so he borrows it from Bob at 10%. Carl agrees to pay Bob a total of $550 (principal and interest).

Sometime later, Carl pays back $500 of the $550. Bob now has his $1,000 back and is awaiting his remaining $50 in interest. But the $1,000 represents all the money in their world. Where will Carl get the remaining $50?

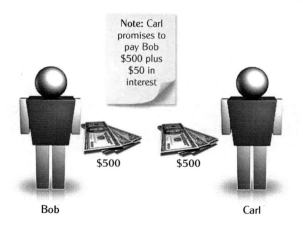

**FIGURE 7A: Carl borrowed $500 at 10% from Bob.
Carl now owes Bob $500 in principal and $50 in interest (annually)**

So Carl can do one of two things: He can work for Bob in place of paying him the $50, or he can borrow the money from Bob to pay him back.

Let's consider the latter. Once again, Carl borrows $500 at 10% interest. He again agrees to pay Bob $550 (principal and interest), in addition to the original $50 in unpaid interest. Carl now owes Bob a total of $600.

Sometime later, Carl pays Bob $500 and has $100 of unpaid interest still to pay. However, Bob has the entire $1,000 that exists in their world. As before, Carl has no way of paying Bob the remaining $100, and once again, he has two choices: work for Bob or borrow more money.

By now, I hope you see that as long as Carl keeps borrowing money from Bob, he will owe more and more until the point where he will *have* to work for Bob.

The point of the story above is that as long as someone charges interest, this "created" money does not really exist; therefore, at some point someone will have to work for it (or keep borrowing money until they work for it).

One can argue that someone could borrow the money, create something of value, such as bake some bread, and profit from it. That is true. But the cost of money (the interest) is being passed along to the ultimate consumer of that product. So the consumer ultimately pays for that interest through borrowing more or working for it. They have to work hard for that "created" money.

I recommend that you think this all the way through. It's not easy. But at the core of it, we end up with the three teams: consumer, producer, and banker.

The consumer borrows money from the banker and pays interest.

The producer borrows money from the banker, creates a product or service, and passes the interest to the consumer, which ultimately means the consumer pays for the interest along with profits to the producer.

Yes, there is value to the consumer. But let's focus on the money flow here.

Ultimately, the consumer pays for all scenarios by eventually working for the banker or borrowing more money, which gets him into more debt, resulting in him working even more for the banker. Under these circumstances, it should be no surprise that with many couples both parties have to work and are still barely making it. It also helps to explain why 34.5% of the average American's income goes to financial institutions to cover interest alone – they're working for the banker!

Now, that might seem unfair. Well, there are several ways to look at this. At the end of the day, the consumer is getting something of value and is willing to work for it. There's nothing wrong with that.

> **Banks create new money with interest.**
> **Someone has to borrow more money**
> **or work to pay this off.**

Let's take this to an extreme. The Federal Reserve System is a form of bank. It's privately held, not a government entity. They charge interest on money they lend to banks, and this interest is passed on to the public (consumers and producers). That means every consumer in the country has to work (or borrow) to pay off the "Fed" in some way. They are the ultimate bankers.

So, what's the point of all of this? It's quite simple.

Every time you charge interest as a private lender, you "create new money" that did not exist before, and someone has to pay it off by either borrowing more money or by working for it. This is the reality of the world.

But Wait! There's More!

As a banker, it's important that you spend time to understand how money works, as described in the previous section. Let's look at how the monetary system works.

In the past, a paper dollar was backed by gold or silver. Now, it's not; it's backed by a promise of the government. That's what is known as "fiat" currency. A paper dollar can be redeemed only for another paper dollar.

Money is truly debt, and if there were no debt, there would be no money. The importance of this is very significant, and the details are beyond the scope of this book. Please refer to the Resources page in the back of this book for more information, or we can refer you to additional videos found on our website.

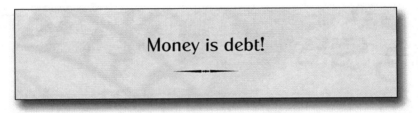

Money is debt!

Being a Private Lender

Imagine being in this business. Your company:

- Takes little risk and shifts it to others
- Makes more money with less work than most other companies
- Always gets paid first
- Needs no money of its own
- Borrows all the money it needs at very little cost
- Lends out the money and shifts the risk to the borrowers
- Has consumers fighting to lend you money at 1% or less when inflation is five times that
- Offers only the *belief* that the money is safe

What a business!

Obviously, we're talking about banking. But what if I said you can mimic the same process and make money like a bank? If you could make money without having to get a "banking license," without having to be rich, without anyone checking your credit, would you want to?

People are doing it every day. People that have discovered the "code" are doing it and generating great passive income, just like the bank.

The power comes from that one, single word that allows the average person to implement the banker's code – and it's 100% legal! The word is "hypothecation."

Hypothecation takes place when a borrower pledges collateral to secure a debt. When a property owner pledges property as collateral for a mortgage, that's hypothecation. Now the bank has a loan that's secured by the property. They can turn around and reuse that loan (a piece of paper) and pledge it as collateral for their own loan. That's called "re-hypothecation." And that's precisely where banks shine, and anyone that understands that can as well.

The most important word in banking is "hypothecation."
From that comes another word bankers use: "re-hypothecation."

Where do you start? Simple. Begin with an understanding of the three key things all bankers always need to do.

Three Things Bankers Do

Bankers have to do three things. They cannot skip any of these steps, because that could negatively affect their business. The steps are:

- Use leverage (OPM – other people's money).
- Find borrowers. Without borrowers, they can't make money.
- Do relatively safe loans secured by assets. Bankers are always about safety; they're not in the business of taking risks.

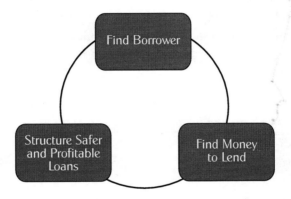

FIGURE 8: **Three things bankers must always do**

As a private lender, these things can be automated. But it's important that you never miss any of those steps.

> The three things lenders do are: (1) find borrowers, (2) find money to lend out, and (3) structure safer and profitable loans.

Banker Versus Private Lender

As you are discovering, bankers have a lot of power. They set the rules, they do the least amount of work, they take the least risk, and they make a lot of money.

The good news is that average individuals (i.e., private lenders) can implement the same secrets and strategies the bankers use. A private lender (in this book) is an individual that implements the Banker's Code – the same strategies banks use to make money. A private lender makes money just like the bank, but without the hassles of having a brick-and-mortar bank, licensing requirements, and employees. Strip all that away, and what's left are the money-making strategies.

If you're ready, let's get started.

"So it's making money just like the bank," said Dr. Jazz excitedly. "It's about using the same finance principles the banks use. These principles exist, and anyone can use them. You do not need to open a real bank or get a banking license."

"Does everyone know that? I mean, I had no idea this was the case," I uttered.

"People should know this, but they choose not to. In fact, the educational system was set up to avoid teaching how money truly works," Dr. Jazz said as he stood up. "Let's walk around the plaza, and you can ask me whatever you wish."

"And the charging of interest," I continued as we walked, "seems to force others to borrow more money – or work for it. That's something I've never, ever heard before."

"Hopefully, you now get what Albert Einstein meant when he said, 'Those who understand interest, earn it; those who don't, pay it.' He was talking about a banker and consumer. It's very powerful information.

"Let's head to my house for supper," said Dr. Jazz as he turned towards home. As we walked I continued trying to absorb all this information.

"We'll talk along the way about how to make this work for you," he offered.

As we approached his house, Dr. Jazz's many grandchildren ran to him. "Les enfants. Allez les enfants," he laughed heartily and fondly, introducing me to his many family members as he walked me to the dinner table, happy to have the children around him.

The doctor was a man of many surprises. I had no idea he spoke French!

CHAPTER SUMMARY

- Banks create new money with interest. Someone has to borrow more money or work to pay this off.
- The most important word in banking is "hypothecation." From that comes another word bankers use: "re-hypothecation."
- Three things bankers do:
  - Use leverage
  - Find borrowers
  - Do safer and more profitable loans
- Private lenders are individuals that can make money *just like* the bank.

CHAPTER FIVE

The Language Of Bankers

As supper ended, I joked to Dr. Jazz, "I didn't realize you speak French, Dr. Jazz."

He recited something in French with a smile, but I had no idea what he said.

"I speak multiple languages. In fact, all my children do, as well," he replied.

I had just met his wife, France, and his children, Jacqueline, Gisele, Michel, and Pierre, along with a whole lot of grandchildren, all with French names. That should have been a hint! In fact, his wife's name should have been the first clue.

"So, are you French?" I asked.

He chuckled.

"Actually, I'm Lebanese. We all learned three languages as children. But the language you need to learn is the language of bankers. That is your first assignment, and I will give you a list of basic words to learn. You will not appreciate the power of banking until you have this foundation," he said as he wrote some words on a piece of paper and handed it over to me.

It's important to understand and speak the language of bankers. In this chapter, we'll cover these important terms:

- Collateral
- Loan to Value (LTV), Combined Loan to Value (CLTV), and Protective Equity
- Promissory Note
- Secured and Unsecured Loans
- Security Instruments
- Foreclosure
- Leverage
- Arbitrage
- Velocity of Money
- Asset-Based Lender

Wikipedia.org, defines "collateral" this way: "In lending agreements, collateral is a borrower's pledge of specific property to a lender, to secure repayment of a loan. The collateral serves as protection for a lender against a borrower's default – that is, any borrower failing to pay the principal and interest under the terms of a loan obligation."

For the purposes of this book, I primarily use real estate as collateral for our loans. One of the common mistakes is that people think lenders are in the real estate business. They are not. They are in the financing business and simply use real estate as collateral. The collateral does not make the business.

The next terms on the list are LTV, CLTV, and Protective Equity. Let's start with LTV; it stands for "loan to value."

LTV is simply the loan amount divided by the value of the collateral or property. For example, if we loaned someone $65,000 against a property worth $100,000 that has no other loans, the LTV is calculated as follows:

LTV = loan amount/value of property
LTV = $65,000/$100,000
This gives us an LTV of 65%.

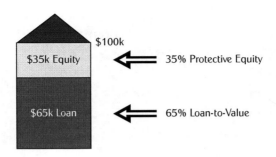

FIGURE 9: A low LTV loan

The remaining 35% is called "protective equity." It's the cushion lenders are looking for in case the borrower fails to pay. As a lender, we want to make sure our LTV is low and the protective equity is high. The LTVs we look for vary depending on the collateral. For example, on a single-family residence, we might decide 65% LTV is the highest we would go. The protective equity of 35% is good. So if the borrower stops paying, the borrower has a lot to lose, and the lender can potentially end up with the property worth $100,000 for which he invested $65,000. The lender feels safer with that.

CLTV stands for "combined loan to value." This is similar to LTV, except the formula looks like this:

CLTV = sum of all loans, including amount to borrow/value of property

Protective equity is all the equity above that loan amount. The formula looks like this:

Protective Equity = 100% − CLTV

So the CLTV is the sum of all existing loans against a property, including the amount the borrower is asking for, divided by the value of the property. For example, if someone borrows $10,000 against a property (single-family residence) worth $100,000 which has an existing loan of $75,000, the CLTV would be as follows:

CLTV = sum of all loans/value of property
CLTV = ($75,000 + $10,000)/$100,000
CLTV = $85,000/$100,000
CLTV = 85%
Protective Equity = 100% − CLTV
Protective Equity = 100% − 85%
Protective Equity = 15%

Given that the CLTV is more than the maximum 65% LTV (from our example above) and the protective equity is less than 35%, we as lenders would not make this loan.

Through the rest of the book I'll use the terms – CLTV and LTV – interchangeably. Simply use the formula for CLTV when doing calculations.

The LTV is one of the most important numbers in lending. It should be a lower number, typically 65% or lower for residential properties (1 to 4 units).

> ## The maximum LTV on a single-family home or residential property (1 to 4 units), should be no more than 65% in most areas and situations.

Download the free, spreadsheet calculator (more instructions found in the Resources page at the end of the book) that helps you easily make these calculations, as well as other tools mentioned in the book.

What is a Promissory Note?

A promissory note is a written promise to pay, or repay, a certain amount of money at a certain time, or in a certain number of installments, or on demand to a named person. It usually provides for payment of interest.

A promissory note is "secured" if there is some collateral of value that secures the loan. For example, let's say that Joe borrows $10,000 from Sam and offers his house as security. If Joe fails to repay Sam, then Sam can go after Joe's house to get his money back. That is called "a secured loan."

An "unsecured" promissory note is simply that, a promissory note that has nothing tangible to back it up. As a private lender, we avoid unsecured promissory notes as much as possible.

When lending money to others, private lenders always prefer secured loans against real estate.

> In this book, we will consider only real estate as collateral for our loans to others.

The person receiving the loan proceeds (borrower) becomes obligated to repay the debt by signing a promissory note, which specifies:

- Amount of the loan (principal)
- Interest rate (interest)
- Amount and frequency of payments
- When the borrower must repay the principal (due date, also known as "maturity date")

- Penalties imposed if the borrower fails to timely pay or tender a payment (late charge), or if the borrower decides to pay a portion or the entire principal prior to the due date (prepayment penalty)

The promissory note also identifies the borrower and the person who will receive the payments (lender or note holder).

If you would like to learn more about completing a promissory note, you can find more and access it from The Banker's Code Tools site (information found on the Resources page).

What Secures Your Investment?

Your investment is secured by a security instrument recorded against the borrower's property. In real estate, there are generally two types of security instruments: a deed of trust and a mortgage. Unlike deposits in a bank or savings and loan, which are generally insured by a federal agency (such as FDIC) and may usually be withdrawn with limited notice, the promissory note:

- Involves some risk to principal (a typical feature of all investments)
- Establishes a specific and predetermined period of time for the repayment of your investment
- Does not benefit from insurance issued by a federal agency

The security instrument (deed of trust or a mortgage) works in conjunction with the promissory note in that it ties the promissory note to the property (the security). So a promissory note by itself, even if the property address is mentioned on it, does not tie it to the property. The security instrument ties the promissory note and property together.

As shown below, think of the promissory note as a borrower saying, "I promise to pay you . . ." and the security instrument saying ". . . and if I don't pay you, here is the collateral you can go after."

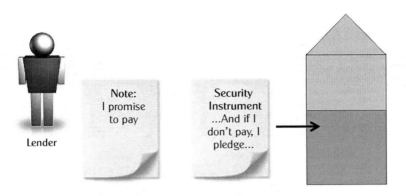

FIGURE 10: A security instrument goes along with a promissory note

As I noted above, in real estate the security instrument can be either a deed of trust or a mortgage. They are essentially the same, except for the type of foreclosure conducted. Foreclosure is the legal process by which the lender repossesses – due to non-payment, typically – the collateral the borrower pledged. There are two types of foreclosure processes available in real estate: judicial and non-judicial.

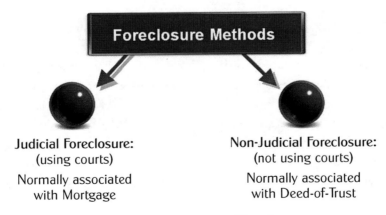

FIGURE 11: Various types of foreclosures

The first process comes from the word "judge" and it means "through the courts." A judicial foreclosure involves the courts and is generally inefficient for lenders. Non-judicial foreclosure, on the other hand, is a lot more efficient for lenders, in that no courts are involved, and the foreclosure is conducted more efficiently (depending on the state).

If you would like to learn more about completing a deed of trust, you can find more information at The Banker's Code Tools site (see the Resources page).

What is Financial Leverage?

Financial leverage is the use of borrowed money, normally used to buy the assets that will generate your cash flow. For example, getting a mortgage to buy a property is financial leverage.

To understand wealth, you need to understand leverage really well.

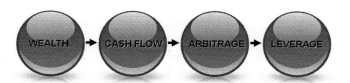

FIGURE 12: Breaking "wealth" into basic components

The fastest way to gain wealth is through financial leverage, the right kind of financial leverage. On the other hand, the fastest way to lose wealth is also with leverage, the wrong kind of leverage. The problem is that many people are using the wrong kind of leverage to build wealth, and they are setting themselves up to lose. In this book, I'll cover the right kind of leverage – positive leverage. For more information on leverage, please refer to my book, *The Wealthy Code*.

What is Arbitrage?

Arbitrage is "the spread" between the rate at which you borrow money, and the rate you gain from investing that money. For example, if you borrow money at 6% and invest it at 9%, you will be making a 3% spread. That's called "arbitrage." Cash flow is generated through spreads (or arbitrage). Arbitrage is known as a "leveraged" strategy since it involves borrowed money. Arbitrage is the lifeblood of banking.

Velocity of Money

This is one of those terms that every banker knows and most consumers have never heard.

According to Investopedia.com, Velocity of Money is ". . . a term used to describe the rate at which money is exchanged from one transaction to another. Velocity is important for measuring the rate at which money in circulation is used for purchasing goods and services. This helps investors gauge how robust the economy is. It is usually measured as a ratio of GNP to a country's total supply of money."

That's a definition for the entire economy.

However, another definition applies more specifically to us. I like to think of velocity of money as the "turning of the same money." In other words, for the same money, as you "turn" it, you acquire more and more assets or profits. By "turning," I mean investing the money and then retrieving it.

Let's consider an example in real estate.

Suppose you have $100,000 in investment capital, and you're considering three investments. (To keep things simple, assume all other things are equal – risk and reward).

> **Property A:** You can use the $100,000 as a down payment and collect $400 per month in positive cash flow.

> **Property B:** You can buy and hold for the long term in a historically strong, appreciating area.

Property C: You can buy for $72k and resell immediately for a small profit.

Let's consider property A. This looks like a good deal. But, once your capital is invested, you can't invest in anything else until you retrieve it at some point in the future. With property B, it might take you years to get your money back, but that $100,000 might translate to a lot more equity in five years.

However, property C allows you to retrieve the money relatively soon while making an immediate profit. You can keep using the same strategy for "turning" this money and making small profits, say $10,000 at a time. With the other properties (A and B), you also have the potential of lost opportunity cost for not having the capital in place (i.e., missing out on a great opportunity by not having the capital on hand).

This applies to a lot more than just real estate. Here is another example.

You have access to the $100,000 line of credit. You lend it out secured by real estate at 65% LTV. As the borrower pays you back, you lend that money out ASAP. You don't want to keep money sitting around doing nothing – what we call "dead" money. What's the effect of that? Your internal rate of return gets higher. Even though you might be lending money at a certain interest rate, your yield (return) for that year is higher because of velocity of money. The net effect is that as you "velocitize" money, in effect, you are allowing your money to grow!

With velocity of money, your return (yield) goes up. So if a borrower is paying you 12% and you keep that money "turning" by lending it out as soon as you get it, your return over time goes up. So you will be receiving 13% when they are paying you 12%, due to velocity! This concept is further developed in Chapter 8.

Now, let's make this a little more interesting.

How can we generate more passive income using velocity of money?

Imagine a scenario where you can invest money into acquiring an income-producing asset, get your capital back in 90 days, and have recurring passive income for years to come from that income-producing asset, with your money comfortably back in your pocket 90 days later, or sooner. Can you do that again and again?

Absolutely. In fact, banks do it all the time.

In conclusion, velocity of money is an important concept to consider in your investments. Savvy investors consider this first in their due diligence. How fast can I get my money back to reinvest? You should, too.

Asset-Based Lending

In simple terms, asset-based lending (ABL) is lending money secured by assets. In general, asset-based lenders look at the asset first and make sure there's enough collateral to cover the loan. Many financial institutions lend based on a borrower's ability to pay first, which is different.

The lending covered in this book is ABL. We believe it's a safer position to take; always make sure there is enough collateral to cover the loan. With this type of lending, there are two very important numbers: one is the LTV (mentioned previously in this chapter), and the second is the value of the asset. These two numbers serve as the foundation of our lending. Later, we'll add our underwriting criteria to help make this a safer loan.

> In asset-based lending, the two most important numbers are the LTV and the value of the asset. This is in addition to a good underwriting criteria.

I reviewed the terms on the piece of paper.

This was a good review, I thought confidently. I had gone through these the last time with my mentor during The Wealthy Code *lessons. I was so excited about all that I was learning from Dr. Jazz.*

But even more, I was fascinated by the manuscript and the secrets it revealed daily. I loved the way Dr. Jazz handled its pages and the musty smell that inevitably followed it around.

"You must be ready to accept what I'm going to tell you next," the doctor said, "but I'm guessing it will be easier for you than for most people. Ah, I see you want to look more in the manuscript, but you will have to wait until later."

We walked towards his home as the sun set, and I left with endless possibilities racing through my mind.

CHAPTER SUMMARY

- Make sure you know the basic terms of lending.

CHAPTER SIX

The Banker's Mindset

"WHY DO YOU THINK MINDSET IS SO IMPORTANT? IT JUST SEEMS THAT TALK-ing about it is such a waste of time," I questioned Dr. Jazz.

"George, you have been an entrepreneur since you were 16, and because you ran several businesses with your dad, you cannot relate to what many people go through. Mindset is the difference between success and failure. Most people struggle with simply taking action, while you might take action, run with this information, and make it a reality.

"A winning mindset comes from your beliefs. Your beliefs come from your childhood, and so your limiting beliefs affect your mindset. However, in this case, we are talking about the banker's mindset.

"This is probably the hardest mindset to adopt because it goes against the investor's mindset."

If you want to be successful as a private lender, the thing that will have the biggest impact is adopting the banker's mindset. Many of us bounce between an investor's mindset and a consumer's mindset. A banker's mindset is foreign to most of us. In fact, it takes most people years to adopt; some, however, get it almost instantly!

As a private lender, the difference between success and failure starts with the mindset – the banker's mindset. Investors have a different reality, different beliefs. That's why it's challenging for some to become "bankers." They've been conditioned to think like an investor or consumer, not a banker. But once they see things through the banker's eyes, they see a whole different world.

Let's start with this. For every dollar you have, you can earn interest on it, or you can give up the interest you would have earned on it (if, for instance, you spent it or put it under a mattress).

Take a minute, read that again, and then put down the book and think about it. Think about that money you spent earlier on lunch. That could have earned you a *lot* of interest over the years. You gave it up.

This is called opportunity cost. Every time you hold a dollar, recognize that you can be earning interest on it (it can be working for you), or you can give up all that money it would have earned for you by spending it or hiding it under your mattress.

Now, I'm not saying you have to be frugal or anything like that. I'm simply letting you know that a banker always looks at the interest everything can make them. That's it.

Just like business owners think of their employees as working hard to make them money, bankers see dollar bills as little employees working hard to make them money.

After all, bankers are in the money business. They are masters in understanding risk and shifting risk away from them. Bankers make more money while taking on less risk! They also know how to use other people's money to make money.

Bankers also know that they need to keep the money moving. They use the velocity of money to make even more. They recommend that we save our money in their savings accounts, CDs, etc., all of which is dead money, money that's not moving. But for the bankers, it's money they can move – or velocitize.

Bankers want their money to be
moving constantly; i.e., out in loans.
However, they want to make sure
depositors don't move *their* money on
them, so they ask the depositors to keep
their money idle in the savings accounts
or Certificates of Deposit. This allows
the bankers to move that "dead" money
and make more money with it.

Banks need borrowers to borrow their money. They also work with customers (other people's money) that trust them. All of this will make sense as we start combining it a little later.

Bankers Make the Rules

Remember the modern Golden Rule? "He who has the gold makes the rules." Here's an updated version that applies to bankers: "He who is *perceived* to have the gold makes the rules." Why "perceived"? Because bankers are simply using *other* people's money to lend and are using that power of access to money to make the rules.

As a banker, you'll start acting like you make the rules, and then you *will* make the rules! You'll write the rules for other investors to follow.

The Mindset of an Investor Versus that of a Banker

Investors hang on to equity – bankers hang on to money. Which one makes more sense?

If you think the former is more important, please revisit *The Wealthy Code*. It's the latter – money – you need to be hanging on to.

Bankers never forget this; they're in the money business.

THE INVESTOR'S MINDSET	THE BANKER'S MINDSET
Investors hang on to equity to show their net worth.	Bankers want investors to keep their equity because it makes the bankers shift more risk to the investor and less to the banker (i.e., they need that protective equity to keep their loan safer by having a lower LTV loan).
Investors like to own properties.	Bankers use properties as collateral to secure their cash flow. They dislike owning them.
Investors are in the landlording business.	Bankers are in the money business.
Investors generate cash flow by using bankers' money and owning properties.	Bankers make money by using consumers' money and collateralizing by the mortgages they get when lending the money out.
Investors make a down payment to buy properties and, therefore, shift the risk away from the lender and onto themselves.	Bankers require a down payment from the borrowers to shift more risk to the borrowers and away from the banker.
Asset rich, cash poor.	Asset rich and cash rich.
Investors must have good credit and financials to qualify for loans.	Bankers need not have good credit or financials.

FIGURE 13: Comparing the investor's and banker's mindsets

Risk Relationship with Borrower

Assume the following scenario (shown below):

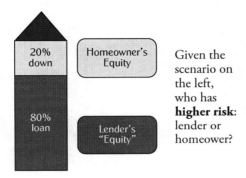

FIGURE 14: Who's taking the higher risk?

A homeowner decides to buy a $100,000 house. He gets a loan from a lender for 80% of a property ($80,000), making a 20% down payment ($20,000). Whose money is at a higher risk? The homeowner's or the lender's?

Let's consider this. If the homeowner had to sell the property the very next day, he would have to pay the lender the $80,000 loan first, then pay off closing costs and commissions, leaving him with $10,000 to $12,000 from his $20,000 down payment.

Therefore, the homeowner's money is at a higher risk because their money is affected first, before the lender's.

The lender was in the safer position. The homeowner took the higher risk.

> **A down payment on a property is in a higher risk position than a lender's money.**

Now, consider the scenario below:

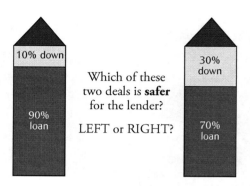

FIGURE 15: Which scenario is safer for the lender?

Assume these two transactions involve the same property. For the property on the left, the lender provides a 90% loan, and the homeowner puts 10% down. With the property on the right, the lender provides a 70% loan, and the homeowner puts 30% down. Which is safer for the lender?

The answer is that the lender prefers the deal on the right – lending less money.

The lender in the example at right has more cushion if the property value goes down. The lender is better off providing a smaller amount toward the full price of the property. By doing that, the lender shifted the risk away from them and towards the homeowner.

The scenario on the left, where the homeowner put only 10% down, is better for the homeowner because they have less to lose. By doing that, the homeowner shifted more risk toward the lender. (Even though the homeowner is still in a riskier position, they shifted some of the risk towards the lender.)

Now, consider this scenario (below):

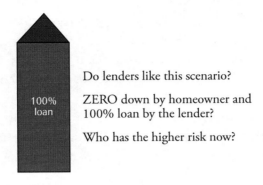

Do lenders like this scenario?

ZERO down by homeowner and 100% loan by the lender?

Who has the higher risk now?

FIGURE 16: Is this a favorable position for the lender?

Do lenders like to put up 100% of the loan while the homeowner puts nothing down? What happens if the homeowner walks away from this? The lender gets all the risk. So in this case, the lender shifted the risk away from the homeowner and towards them.

This is the scenario that happened in the late 2000s and is the reason many property owners walked away. They had nothing to lose (they had no down payment). The lenders shifted the risk away from the homeowners and towards themselves.

Now, consider this scenario:

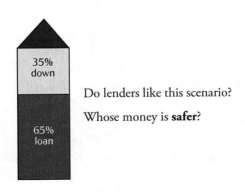

Do lenders like this scenario?

Whose money is **safer**?

FIGURE 17: Would lenders like this scenario?

What about the situation where the lender provides a 65% LTV loan. Do lenders like this? Of course they do. If the homeowner defaults, the lender could potentially get 100% of the property for 65% of the value. The lender could get 100% of the equity, and the 35% equity is a nice cushion. It's the protective equity. Once again, the lender has shifted a lot more risk towards the homeowner and away from them.

What's common to all these scenarios? The risk relationship between the lender and the property owner. The lender and the property owner both recognize there is risk in such transactions. Bankers, however, shift most of it to property owners. They are masters in shifting the risk.

LENDER RISK   BORROWER RISK

FIGURE 18: Borrower/lender risk relationship

If the lender's risk goes up, the borrower's risk goes down, and vice-versa. They never go in the same direction.

LENDER RISK   BORROWER RISK

FIGURE 19: Borrower/lender risk relationship

Risk is always being shifted away from, or towards, one of the two parties. The question to consider is, in which direction do *you* want the risk to be pointing? Do you want to take on more risk or less?

As the lender's loan to value (LTV) goes down (and the property owner's equity goes up), more risk is shifted away from the lender and onto the property owner. In the previous example of the 65% LTV, the lender shifted more risk towards the borrower and away from themselves.

> **Bankers are masters in shifting much of the risk to the borrower.**
>
> **There is always a risk relationship between the borrower and the lender. One of the ways a lender shifts more of the risk to the borrower is by lowering the LTV.**

Example of Bob and Ivan

Consider the story of Banker Bob and Investor Ivan. Ivan is considering buying a single-family home, fixing it, and then selling it in 6 months for a profit. Ivan then decides to discuss this with Banker Bob. After about 10 minutes of introducing themselves, here is how the conversation and their thought processes went:

Ivan: I need to borrow $80,000, Bob. The property is worth $100,000 right now ("as is" value), and I'm buying it for $75,000. Fixed up, it's worth $150,000.

Ivan's thoughts: I really need this money to be able to generate a good profit. I wish this banker knew how good this deal was and how many similar deals I've done. He should just lend it to me, no questions asked.

Bob: Ivan, do you have any other collateral besides this home that you're willing to pledge?

Bob's thoughts: He has good financials. I really want to tie up everything I can to make sure this is a secure deal for me. What else can I ask from this guy to make my loan more secure?

Ivan: I have another rental property – a duplex – and it's free and clear. I included it in my loan application; it's on my balance sheet right here, worth $120,000.

Ivan's thoughts: Hopefully, that should do it. . . .

Bob: I think we can work this out, Ivan. So, if you're willing to pledge the property you're buying and the duplex you own free and clear, with your financials I think we should be able to make it work. The only caveat is, are you willing to take $68,300?

Bob's thoughts: This is looking good. Let me try to make it even safer by shifting more risk to him. I've tied up extra collateral; I'll try to have him put more money into the deal and me less. I've already shifted a lot of the risk to him.

Ivan: Would $75,000 work?

Ivan's Thoughts: I can squeeze my contractors a little and make it work with $75,000. But I don't want to share this with the banker.

Bob: Ivan, let me see what I can do … (takes his calculator to another room).

Ivan's Thoughts: Should I have accepted the $68,300? Hmmm. I *can* make this work with that, and I'd prefer $68,300 to nothing. Maybe I should wait. But will it be too late?

Bob: Ivan, we can make it work at $72,400, but at 1% higher. Meaning we can do $72,400 at 8%, not 7%.

The story above depicts the dance between investors and bankers. Bankers want to shift as much risk to the investor as possible. Investors want to borrow money for their deals and are willing to give up a lot for that. Bankers ultimately make the rules – they tie up all the collateral – and end up making a lot more money than the investor, and with peace of mind. The investors' stress levels go up significantly for the duration of their projects because they have a lot to lose for the potential money they could make.

Banking is About Safety

So to summarize, the Number 1 rule of banking is safety. They shift the risk to the borrower. They are in the financing game, not the investing game. They dislike risks. And what's interesting is that they end up making more money than the investors they finance.

They finance the risks of others. They allow investors to take the risks while the bankers tie up all the collateral and take a safer position.

"This is fascinating. But why wouldn't they just do a real estate deal like an investor and make money like that?" I questioned.

"Well, George, you haven't seen the best part yet. Once you do, you will understand what I mean when I say that they are in the financing game, not the investing game," Dr. Jazz smiled.

"Let me ask you this, George. How would you like to 'clone' money and create spreads as much as you want? How would you like to do all that by simply using paper, without dealing with the hassles of properties, businesses, or physical structures?" he continued.

"What do you mean?" I questioned.

He deftly pushed another pebble out of the pathway with the toe of his shoe and said, "Let's suppose you have $20,000 in cash. How would you like to clone this $20,000 three, four, or even ten times, in fact as many times as you want, and make a nice spread off of that?"

"Is this legal?" I asked.

Dr. Jazz threw his head back and laughed aloud.

"Of course. This is the secret to banking. I hope you are starting to see why bankers keep this a secret. But we're jumping ahead. Let's talk about something else. Any questions first?"

CHAPTER SUMMARY

- Bankers are masters in *shifting* risk to borrowers.
- Bankers focus on covering the downside and letting the upside take care of itself.
- A down payment on a property is in a higher risk position than a lender's money.
- For every dollar you have, you can earn interest on it, or you can give up the interest you would have earned on it.
- Bankers see every dollar as a little salesperson making them money (interest).
- Bankers make the rules.

Refer to the Resources page for a free bonus chapter with Dr. Jazz.

CHAPTER SEVEN

But Who Would Pay 12%?

"DR. JAZZ," I SAID HESITANTLY, "I DO HAVE A FEW QUESTIONS. YOU MEN-tioned that borrowers will pay private investors 10%, 12%, or even more. Why would they do that when they can borrow money directly from a real bank?"

Before we go on, let me answer some questions you probably have.

Why Would Anyone Pay 10%, 12%, or Even More?

Let's assume you found a real estate deal worth $500,000 you could purchase directly from the bank for $250,000. Assume, also, that you had 10 days to close this deal. You know you could turn around and sell this property within 6 months. Only one small problem: you don't have the money.

Here are three possibilities:

1. You can ignore the deal because you don't have the money.

2. You can go to a traditional bank to get financing, knowing they would take a minimum of 30 days to check all your financials,

credit, and other details, while limiting your number of loans to four or less, among the million other limitations they have, just to get a loan for 6% that requires you to put down 30%.

3. You can get the money from a private money lender at 12%, 14%, or even more knowing that you will not have to go through the same process as a traditional bank (since this lender is an asset-based lender), and they can close within the 10 days you need.

Obviously, option no. 3 is a good one, but how much is the interest truly costing? If the interest is 12% for 6 months, the interest is $15,000 for that period. For the same amount in selection no. 2, the 6% interest for the same period would cost $7,500.

So for a difference of $7,500, this borrower can go with selection no. 3, close the deal much more easily, and make a potential profit of more than $200,000. Without that option, the borrower would have lost the potential profit.

And going back to the question, why would someone pay 12%, 14%, or more? Because of the potential profit they can have, knowing the difference in interest is minimal (given the profit) for such a short-term deal.

Can anyone do this? Yes! As long as they have the right education.

Is this risky? Look around you. Almost every corner of the United States, and the world for that matter, holds a bank. The biggest buildings are banks. That tells you the business model works. So is it risky? Everything you do without educating yourself is risky. Most people think putting money in mutual funds is safe and doesn't require a lot of education! Think again!

Why haven't I heard of this before? Banking has been around for a long, long time. So has private lending. In fact, some of the top executives in the San Francisco Bay area, where I learned about this, are doing it. You haven't heard of it because it's still the game of the rich. Everyone thinks you have to have money to do this, but you don't. It does help to have some money, but it can be done without it.

Can I do this without money or good credit? Yes! The key to this whole thing is that word again: "hypothecation"!

"These are good questions," Dr. Jazz said as he opened the big leather book.

"One more thing, George. Once you decide to start doing this, and you want your spouse to listen and pay strict attention to every word you say, talk in your sleep," he joked. I laughed, thinking of his wife, France, and her tolerance of his jokes.

"I know you wish to study this book in more depth. It's not that I don't trust you, my friend," Dr. Jazz said quietly. "But there is a time and a place ...and it is soon." He looked off into the distance and then quickly laughed.

"It's time for your next lesson and my next supper. Let's see what France has for us, and we can play with les enfants *while we talk."*

CHAPTER SUMMARY

- Banking has been around for a long time for a good reason – the business model works!
- Borrowers are willing to pay more to access money quickly without going through the traditional banks. To them, it's not about the cost of money as much as the speed and ease of getting the money because of access to opportunities.

Refer to the Resources page for a free bonus chapter with Dr. Jazz.

CHAPTER EIGHT

The Finance: It Gets Better

DR. JAZZ SLOWLY OPENED THE MANUSCRIPT TO A PAGE ENTITLED, "IDEAS for Widening the Spreads Through Finance." The page was filled with diagrams, arrows, calculations and notes. Dr. Jazz said, "Herbert was intrigued by how one could increase one's spread. That means, increasing your returns and lowering the cost of money without changing either!"

"So what does that mean in English?" I smiled.

"Well, imagine someone pays you 12% and you pay your source of money 8%. The spread is 4%, the difference between 12% and 8%. Now imagine that the person pays you 12%, but you receive 13%. And when you pay your source of money 8%, they receive 8%, but you pay them 7%. The spread now goes from 4% to 6%. You are making 13% and paying 7%," Dr. Jazz said cautiously, checking to make sure I got it.

"Huh? How's that?"

With a big smile, he said, "I'll explain. But it gets better."

And he pointed to the page….

The spread between the cost of borrowed money, i.e., the cost of money, and the return, is typically a small percentage. For example, if you borrowed money at 6% and loaned it out at 9%, you would make 3%. However, using some creative finance, it's possible to increase that.

Let's first consider the return on a loan.

Return on Investment

Earlier, I explained velocity of money. I mentioned that with velocity of money, your internal rate of return (think of this as return) gets higher. Let's look at an example. Assume two lenders, David and Steve, lend out $60,000. Let's assume the loan terms are as follows: $5,600 per month for 12 months. Here's what the schedule will look like.

PAYMENT#	DAVID	STEVE (the smart one)
1	$5600	$5600
2	$5600	$5600
3	$5600	$5600
4	$5600	$5600
5	$5600	$5600
6	$5600	$5600
7	$5600	$5600
8	$5600	$5600
9	$5600	$5600
10	$5600	$5600
11	$5600	$5600
12	$5600	$5600
TOTAL	$67,200	$67,200

FIGURE 20: David and Steve's streams of income from private lending

They both started with $60,000 and ended up with $67,200 after 12 months. That's a 12% return. (Advanced investors will say the yield is higher, but let's keep this simple.)

70

David decides to leave his monthly payments in the bank until he receives all his payments. So, by the end of the 12 months, he would have $67,200.

Steve, the smart lender, decides to "turn his money" by lending it out as soon as he gets it back. When he receives the first payment of $5,600, he lends it out at 12% for 11 months, thus receiving $56 per month for 11 months (refer to the table below).

PAYMENT #	DAVID	STEVE (stream #1)	STEVE (stream #2)
1	$5600	$5600	
2	$5600	$5600	$56
3	$5600	$5600	$56
4	$5600	$5600	$56
5	$5600	$5600	$56
6	$5600	$5600	$56
7	$5600	$5600	$56
8	$5600	$5600	$56
9	$5600	$5600	$56
10	$5600	$5600	$56
11	$5600	$5600	$56
12	$5600	$5600	$56
TOTAL	$67,200	$67,200	$616

FIGURE 21: David and Steve's streams of income from private lending

Steve ends up receiving $67,200 and the $616, resulting in a sum of $67,816. That's a return of 13.03% while David is getting 12%. But Steve doesn't stop there. He does the same thing for the next $5,600 payment as well, resulting in another stream of income of $56 per month. He then does a 10-month loan with that money.

PAYMENT #	DAVID	STEVE (stream #1)	STEVE (stream #2)	STEVE (stream #3)
1	$5600	$5600		
2	$5600	$5600	$56	
3	$5600	$5600	$56	$56
4	$5600	$5600	$56	$56
5	$5600	$5600	$56	$56
6	$5600	$5600	$56	$56
7	$5600	$5600	$56	$56
8	$5600	$5600	$56	$56
9	$5600	$5600	$56	$56
10	$5600	$5600	$56	$56
11	$5600	$5600	$56	$56
12	$5600	$5600	$56	$56
TOTAL	$67,200	$67,200	$616	$560

FIGURE 22: David and Steve's streams of income from private lending. Steve is using velocity of money to make more money.

Steve ends up receiving three streams of income: $67,200, $616, and $560, resulting in a sum of $68,376. That's a return of 13.96% when David is getting 12%. But once again, Steve doesn't stop there. He does the same thing for every $5,600 payment he receives as well, which results in another stream of income of $56 per month for each one. He does that every single month, and in fact, his return keeps going up as he continues to do so.

PAYMENT #	DAVID	STEVE (stream #1)	STEVE (stream #2)	STEVE (stream #3)	STEVE (stream #4)
1	$5600	$5600			
2	$5600	$5600	$56		
3	$5600	$5600	$56	$56	
4	$5600	$5600	$56	$56	$56
5	$5600	$5600	$56	$56	$56
6	$5600	$5600	$56	$56	$56
7	$5600	$5600	$56	$56	$56
8	$5600	$5600	$56	$56	$56
9	$5600	$5600	$56	$56	$56
10	$5600	$5600	$56	$56	$56
11	$5600	$5600	$56	$56	$56
12	$5600	$5600	$56	$56	$56
TOTAL	$67,200	$67,200	$616	$560	$504

FIGURE 23: David and Steve's streams of income from private lending.
Steve is using velocity of money to make more money.

David: $67,200 (12.00% return)
Steve: $67,200 + $616 + $560 + $504 = $68,880 (14.80% return)

The only difference between David, who is now getting 12%, and Steve, who is getting a much higher return, is that Steve is using velocity of money. In fact, his strategy is simple. As soon as money gets into his bank account, he lends it out. Sometimes the money might sit idle for a few months, but Steve lends it as soon as he gets a chance.

In fact, if you think about the above statement carefully, you realize that Steve is even re-lending the $56 right back out as soon as he gets it, making money on that money as well!

> ## Velocity of money increases your returns.

Now, the reality is that you might not be able to lend out the money immediately, as stated earlier. It might sit idle for a few months. There are two ways to address that.

One reason it sits idle is that the amount of money in the bank is small. However, one can tap into the new and exciting peer-to-peer lending on the Internet. This allows anyone to lend money to others for as little as $25 to $50 and get a good return on that. This type of lending is unsecured lending, meaning there is no collateral backing up the loan – riskier than lending secured by collateral, which is the lending I recommend.

However, there is a more elegant solution for money sitting idle in an account until it is lent out. This principle is genius, and it results in lowering the cost of borrowed money!

Lowering the Cost of Borrowed Money

Let's go through some scenarios here:

Scenario 1:

You have $5000 and TWO buckets.

Where would you put the $5000?

FIGURE 24: Into which bucket would you put the $5000?

Let's say you have $5,000 and two buckets: one bucket pays 1%, and the other bucket pays you 6% (shown above). In which bucket would you put your money? This is not a trick question. Obviously, bucket number 2, paying 6%.

Scenario 2:

You have $5000 and TWO buckets.

| 1% | | 6% |

Checking
(EARNING)

LOC
$8,000 debt
(SAVING)

Where would you put the $5000?

FIGURE 25: Into which of these buckets would you put the $5000?

Let's say that you have the same $5,000 and two buckets (above): one bucket pays 1%, and the other bucket saves 6%. Bucket 1 is a checking account where you're earning 1% interest (if you're lucky) and paying taxes on the interest you earn. The second bucket is a line of credit with $8,000 debt. If you place the $5,000 there, you're saving 6% interest on the $5,000 you would have had to pay. So bucket 1 earns you 1%, while bucket 2 saves you 6%.

So where would you put the $5,000? Bucket 1 or 2?

Consider bucket 2. If you placed the $5,000 there, is it liquid (meaning, do you still have access to the money if it goes into the line of credit)? Of course. It's better to place the $5,000 into bucket 2, because while it's sitting there for the few weeks (or months) before you pay your bills or lend the money again, you've saved 6% for those few weeks. You didn't have to pay taxes on the savings.

So saving 6% is equivalent to earning 6% tax-free.

Now, let's see from the bank's perspective what happened. If you had deposited the money into the checking account, the bank would have paid you 1% on $5,000 ($50 per year). But you would have paid them 6% on the $8,000 ($480 per year). That would have resulted in the bank making $430 per year from you. On the other hand, by putting your money in the line of credit, you would have paid the bank 6% on $3,000 ($180) and received nothing from the bank from the checking account. In essence, they made $180, not $480. That $300 went into your pocket! That's the same money most Americans are paying the banks without even knowing it.

But let's get more detailed here. Let's see what's really going on.

Consider the image below. It represents a timeline of 31 days (the horizontal axis). The vertical axis represents the amount of debt on the line of credit. In the diagram below, the debt ranges from $0 to $10,000.

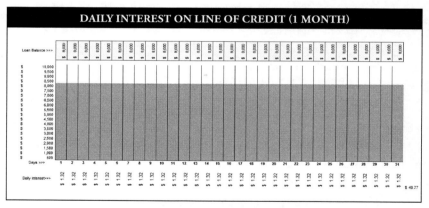

FIGURE 26: Daily interest table

Notice that on day 1 the debt is $8,000. The interest being charged on this day is $8,000 x 6%/365.

The daily interest is calculated as:

Debt x Interest/365

So the daily interest in the diagram is $1.32 for day 1.

If the debt were to remain the same for 31 days, the interest charged for the month would be $40.77. (If you try this on your calculators, you'll get $40.92. For the purposes of this book, I actually rounded up the daily interest rate to $1.32, but I used the actual numbers in the calculation of the monthly sum for $40.77.)

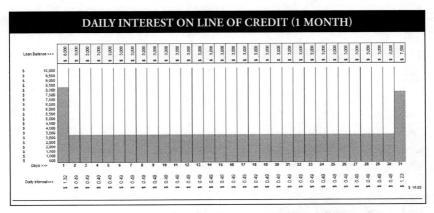

FIGURE 27: Daily interest table

However, if you deposit the $5,000 on day 2, the debt drops to $3,000. The daily interest is $0.49 (49 cents). Assume the debt remains the same (as the $5,000 is sitting idle on the line of credit for 29 days). On the last day, you lend out the $4,500, and the debt goes back up to $7,500. So the interest charged on that day is $1.23. The total for the month is $16.85.

Why is this interesting?

Well, let's look at what, in the line of credit, is the effective interest.

The amount charged on the line of credit would have been $40.77 if the debt had remained at $8,000 and you had deposited the money in a checking account. Therefore, the effective annual interest rate would have been 6%.

By depositing the money into the line of credit, the interest charged was $16.85. This gives you an effective interest of 2.48% and assumes you deposit the $5,000 that you receive in income every month for 29 days.

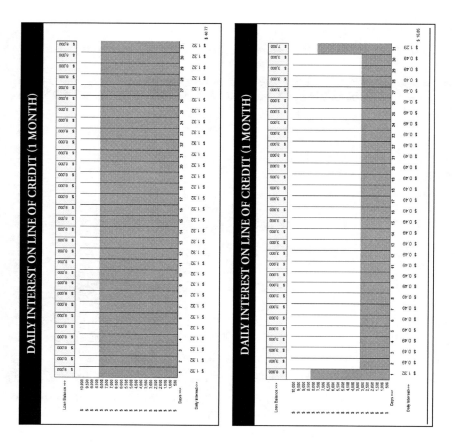

Figure 28: Additional daily interest table

Why is this interesting? Because you effectively lowered the cost of money by depositing your payments into a line of credit while the money sat idle, resulting in a wider spread. Even though on paper our cost of money is 6%, in reality it's 2.48% because of this financing trick. The money that would have gone into the bank's pocket is now being used to lower the effective interest rate!

> Lenders can lower their effective interest rate from borrowed money by using a line of credit in a certain way instead of placing their money in a checking account.

How do you get debt into a line of credit? There are several ways.

The first method is using the line of credit as the source of money you lend out. For example, as you get a loan request, you lend money from that line of credit.

The second method is to borrow the money from another source and use the line of credit to pay it off. As you pay down the line of credit to nothing, you simply write another check to pay off your source of money. In fact, you can use this method to pay off your mortgage. Imagine owning your home free and clear in eight years or less by using your borrower's payments! (Refer to *The Wealthy Code* for more information.)

Let's step back.

By lending money and keeping it turning (using velocity of money), we can increase the yield. Even though our borrower is paying us a specific interest rate, we are receiving a higher return due to velocity of money. And by parking the money in a line of credit at your local bank, you are lowering the effective interest rate. And even though our money source might be charging us a certain interest rate, we are paying them a lower effective interest rate. All this results in a wider spread and more money in your pocket!

"What do you think of that, George?" chuckled Dr. Jazz.

"I'm simply amazed. It's brilliant. This has the touch of genius!" I said as I looked up. I had been hunched over, focused on the book and the diagrams that Dr. Jazz was pointing to. As I stood up and stepped back to stretch my back, I knew my life would never be the same.

"There's more," he said. "There's a lot more, but I'm hesitant to jump into it right now. Your brain will start smoking!" he laughed. "If you think this is good, just wait. It gets much better . . . many, many times better! You see why bankers are the richest people in the world? But soon you will see why they are billionaires."

Dr. Jazz faced me and somberly said, "Knowledge is only the beginning, George. Many responsibilities accompany this knowledge, and soon we will have to talk about them."

I was startled by the look on his face, and he suddenly laughed.

"Enough of that! Let's go see what France has cooked for us and warm ourselves by the fire," he offered as we began to walk towards home.

CHAPTER SUMMARY

- Lenders have access to some powerful financial strategies to boost more profit from a deal.
- One such strategy involves the use of velocity of money, which increases the return by "turning" money as it comes in.
- Lenders can lower their effective interest rate from borrowed money by using a line of credit in a certain way instead of placing their money in a checking account.
- As private lenders become more experienced, there are other financial strategies that can help them boost profit from a deal without charging the borrower more interest.

Refer to the Resources page for a free bonus chapter with Dr. Jazz.

CHAPTER NINE

The Banking: The Parts

THE SUN CLIMBED HIGHER IN THE SKY AS WE SIPPED OUR TEA SLOWLY, savoring the fragrance.

"Have you heard of BOLIs?" asked Dr. Jazz.

"No."

"It stands for Bank Owned Life Insurance, and all banks have them," he explained. "These are a form of life insurance purchased by banks where the bank is the beneficiary and/or the owner.

"Now, why do you suppose they would do that?" he asked.

"Not sure."

"Well, George, let's break the banking system into several parts. Think of your traditional bank. I want to cover each of those parts in a little more detail."

I turned the pages of my notebook to a clean page and grinned as I began to write.

Banking consists of four parts: vehicle, banking, borrower, and depositor.

FIGURE 29: The four parts to banking

Vehicle: the location of the money (the vault) where the money resides. It's where you put your money while it sits in your "banking system." You can have your money in a tin can, in a checking account, in a CD (Certificate of Deposit); wherever you decide to place your money for lending is your vehicle.

Banking: the process – how we lend the money and the methods (the advanced financial strategies) we use to make more money.

Borrower: the person or entity to whom we lend the money.

Depositor: the person (or entity) who saves their money in the bank. This is just one source of money for the bank.

Let's Begin with the Borrower

As a private lender, you need to realize that without borrowers you have no business. Banks don't make money without borrowers. The question is: To whom do we lend?

The answer is simple.

We lend money to anyone we believe is the lowest risk. In the examples in this book, we'll lend money to two types of borrowers: the ones that fit our underwriting criteria and are secured by real estate at 65% LTV (typically one to four units, non-owner occupied) and ourselves. The main focus of Chapter 12 is on lending money to ourselves, which is very different from lending to others.

> ## We lend money to anyone we believe is a low risk.

Let's Talk About the Depositor

Deposits in traditional banks are nothing more than loans to the banks. When banks pay depositors 1%, they're really borrowing that money from them at 1%.

So when talking about depositors, you have to think of them as sources of money and that you are truly borrowing money from them. This means you must comply with all Security and Exchange Commission (SEC) regulations. The SEC is a government agency that protects investors; maintains fair, orderly, and efficient markets; and facilitates capital formation. Whenever you are dealing with raising private money, you have to comply with federal and state securities regulations. Make sure you consult with the right attorney in these matters.

> ## When working with other people's money, always work with the appropriate attorneys. You must comply with all federal and state securities regulations.

Let's divide depositors into three sources: you, friends and family, and strangers.

Of course, you can "deposit" your own money into your own banking system and use that for lending. You can also borrow money from friends and family. Remember, though: Be sure that you comply with all federal and state laws pertaining to borrowing/lending money (beyond the scope of this book).

Let's Talk Next About the Vehicle

Where should you put your money when it's not loaned out? Should you use a regular bank account? Should you use a savings account? You can use any vehicle you choose – a bank account, a tin can, a piggy bank – but the question is: Which vehicle will give you the best performance (i.e., Where will it be safest and grow the most?).

It's important to have the right vehicle. To demonstrate this, let's consider the effects of growing money in a compound manner in three tax environments: taxed, tax-deferred, and tax-free.

Compound interest has been called "The Eighth Wonder of the World" for a good reason – it has the potential to make you rich . . . if you know how to use it. Here's a question. Which of the two choices below would you take?

1) A penny today, double that tomorrow, double that the next day, and so on every day for 30 days.

2) $100,000 today.

Thought about it? Let's look at the numbers. If you selected the daily pennies, here's what you'd get. On day 1 it's $0.01; on day 2 that penny doubles, and you get $0.02, so you now have $0.03; then on day 3, it doubles again, so you get another $0.04. At this point, the $100,000 is looking attractive. But let's keep going.

TAX-FREE COMPOUNDING GROWTH	
DAY	**GROWTH**
1	$ 0.01
2	$ 0.02
3	$ 0.04
4	$ 0.08
5	$ 0.16
6	$ 0.32
7	$ 0.64
8	$ 1.28
9	$ 2.56
10	$ 5.12
...	...
28	$ 1,342,177.28
29	$ 2,684,354.56
30	**$ 5,368,709.12**

FIGURE 30: Tax-free compounding growth table

On day 30 you will receive $5,368,709.12! Now which would you choose? This is obviously compounding growth. In a tax-free environment you would have close to $5.4 million dollars due to compounding.

At this point, you're probably thinking you've heard this before and knew the answer. But let's keep going.

In a taxed environment, assuming a 30% tax bracket, you'd get only $48,196.86! (See table below.) Suddenly the $100,000 seems more attractive. You can see how important a tax-free environment can be.

TAXED COMPOUNDING GROWTH 30% Tax Bracket	
DAY	GROWTH
1	$ 0.01
2	$ 0.02
3	$ 0.03
4	$ 0.05
5	$ 0.08
...	...
28	$ 16,677.11
29	$ 28,351.09
30	$ 48,196.86

FIGURE 31: Taxed compounding growth table with 30% tax bracket

The point of this is that you want your vehicle to be in a tax-advantaged environment to allow compounding to work effectively. What I mean by a "tax-advantaged" environment is something that is either tax-free or tax-deferred. Look for a vehicle that is a tax-advantaged environment.

A "tax-advantaged" environment is something either tax-free or tax-deferred.

Now, let's consider a tax-deferred environment.

TAX-DEFERRED COMPOUNDING GROWTH 30% Tax Bracket	
DAY	GROWTH
1	$ 0.01
2	$ 0.02
3	$ 0.04
4	$ 0.08
5	$ 0.16
...	...
28	$ 1,342,177.28
29	$ 2,684,354.56
30	$ 3,758,096.38

FIGURE 32: Tax-deferred compounding growth table with 30% tax bracket

Simply look at the results: $5,368,709.12; $3,758,096.38; $48,196.86. The only difference was the tax environment! One single decision affects how much money remains in your pocket!

You could use some of the most advanced strategies in banking to make your money grow for you, but placing it in the wrong tax environment will hinder that growth significantly. The vehicle you put your money in is critical.

One of the requirements for the vehicle, therefore, is the need for it to be in a tax-advantaged environment. You might also consider the safety of the money, among other things. The government has given us some favorable environments to use. In fact, big institutions – commercial banking systems – use the same instruments to which we have access. Bank of America, JP Morgan, Chase, Citibank, Wachovia, Wells Fargo, and others deposit (or deposited) tens of billions of dollars of their reserves into high-cash-value life insurance – Bank Owned Life Insurance (BOLI) – for sound economic reasons.

> ## You could use some of the most advanced strategies in banking to make your money grow for you, but placed in the wrong tax environment, growth will be hindered significantly.

It turns out there are a number of vehicles we can use. Which you select is a matter of individual preference. One of the more interesting vehicles turns out to be a certain life insurance, of all things! Banks use it for a reason (BOLI), so what's so compelling about it? The answer is pretty simple. There are two components to permanent life insurance (whole or universal life): the death value and the cash value. As we go through life, we're told that if someone is trying to sell us whole or universal life insurance, we should run away as fast as possible. We've always been told to buy term life insurance and invest the rest. The life insurance companies try to get the death value up and the cash value down. However, it turns out that the cash value of both whole and universal life has some interesting advantages. If you minimize the death benefit and maximize the cash value, you can tap into these advantages:

- It's a tax-advantaged environment.
- Whole life pays dividends every year, allowing us to build cash value quickly; universal life has something similar. Both pay interest every year.
- In some states, the cash value is not accessible to creditors.

And there are additional compelling advantages.

This insurance is structured differently than a regular life insurance agent would do. Insurance agents want to market insurance based on the death benefit. Having a trusted, ethical life insurance agent structure this for you is key. (See Chapter 12 for more on this topic.)

Other vehicles exist for Qualified Retirement Accounts, as well.

Many investors are aware they can do lending in their IRAs, but even better is to invest inside of a Qualified Retirement Plan. The QRP has a lot of advantages that most people are not aware of, as the following table shows.

	SELF-DIRECTED IRA	QUALIFIED RETIREMENT PLAN
Contribution Limit	$5,000 or $6,000 if age 50+	$50,000 or $55,000 if age 50+
Income Restrictions	$125k single or $183k married	None
On-Going Fees	Quarterly plus per transaction	None after initial setup
Ease of Access to Your Cash	Paperwork every time	Easy – you have the checkbook
Speed of Access to Your Cash	2 days to 2 weeks	Instantly – you have the checkbook
Debt Financing Available	No, will be charged UDFI 35% federal tax on % on debt financing	Debt financing OK
Asset Protection	$1 million dollars in bankruptcy	Unlimited protection in bankruptcy, IRS, and creditors
Borrowing	None	$50,000 (or $50% of account, whichever is less)

Details of the Qualified Retirement Plan are beyond the scope of this book. To learn how you can make your private lending tax-free using a QRP, please talk to the appropriate professional or refer to the Resources page in the back of the book.

By choosing the right vehicle, you can increase your money significantly.

Four-Part Harmony

If you create the perfect vehicle but never lend out the money, you've missed the boat. If you do everything else right but place your money in the wrong vehicle, you've missed the boat, as well. You must have all four components working ideally together. The four components together – Vehicle (where the liquid cash for lending resides), Depositor, Borrower, and Banking process – are what makes this waltz flow. The ideal situation will make double-digit returns in a tax-advantaged environment grow in a compounding manner!

Let's Talk Next About the Process

This is the core of a banking system, and it involves three activities. All three activities must be done on an ongoing basis, otherwise the banking system fails. These three activities are:

1. Finding borrowers. Without a borrower, you have no business.

2. Finding money to lend. Without a depositor, you cannot lend.

3. Structuring safer and more-profitable deals.

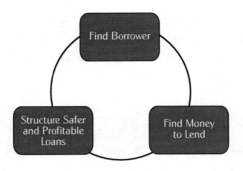

FIGURE 33: The three things private lenders must do

As mentioned before, banking is all about safety. So learning how to structure safer and more-profitable deals is essential in lending. For example, having underwriting criteria, which might include low LTV and specific property types, etc., becomes very important.

"Profitable" can include advanced financial strategies such as velocity of money, leverage, etc. Suffice to say for now that these financial strategies allow you, the banker, to squeeze huge amounts of profit out of every transaction.

"So, who profits from this?" asked Dr. Jazz.

"Hmmm. Depositor? Banker? Borrower? Not sure. Banker?" I offered hesitantly.

"They all profit. However, it's interesting that you say Banker. Where is the Banker here?" he asked me.

"Well, the banker is the one sitting in the bank structuring the loans and taking the deposits," I said.

Dr. Jazz smiled and asked, "Have you ever seen the movie, The Wizard of Oz? *Like the Wizard behind the curtain, the banker is really not seen. He or she is the owner of the bank. He or she makes all the money from the bank, but they have people that take the deposits and approve or disapprove the loans. Do not confuse a teller or a loan officer with the owner of the bank. Tellers and loan officers help the bank owner make money. You* need

91

to be the bank owner. So, you need to have someone that takes the applications for you, handles the appraisals, etc."

"I can't afford all that!" I interrupted. I was angry at the fact that I couldn't afford to hire someone like that. "Most people can't afford this," I sputtered.

CHAPTER SUMMARY

- Banking consists of four parts: Vehicle, Banking, Borrower, and Depositor.
    Vehicle: Where money physically resides while waiting to be lent out
    Banking: The process of lending money
    Borrower: The person or entity to whom you lend money
    Depositor: The person or entity that deposits their money in a bank
- Use a tax-advantaged environment for your money.
- The three activities private lenders do are:
    Find borrowers
    Find money to lend
    Structure safer and profitable deals

Refer to the Resources page for a free bonus chapter with Dr. Jazz.

CHAPTER TEN

The Steps

DR. JAZZ LEANED BACK, CLEARLY DISAPPOINTED IN WHAT I HAD SAID. *He stood up quickly and began walking.* "Come, George. Let's walk."

He looked into the horizon as he spoke, searching for the right words. "Most people are not action-takers, George. Most people find the reason they can't *do* something. These same people live a life of complaining and whining. They want everything given to them on a silver platter," Dr. Jazz pronounced bitterly. "They're not willing to work a little harder and a lot smarter for a better life.

"What you just said made me angry. You concluded something that is not true. You interrupted me with a statement that reflects your own views, your own self-limiting beliefs.

"Let me ask you this: How bad do you want a better life? How hard are you willing to work to have that wonderful life?"

Not waiting for an answer, Dr. Jazz continued. "Life has its ups and downs, its challenges. If you give up when you face a small challenge, you'll always be where you are; you'll never get to that lifestyle you desire. If getting there were easy, everyone would be there. But it's the ones that face their self-limiting beliefs and these challenges that eventually reach their destinations."

"Doctor Jazz," I said, "I still have no money to hire all these people," wanting to justify my previous statement. "But I see what you're saying."

Dr. Jazz was clearly disappointed in me.

"George, the borrower pays these people. Not you." He bowed his head down, disheartened. *"The borrower pays for practically everything. Let me explain...."*

To become a private lender, there are two phases. Phase 1 is the one-time setup of the foundation. Phase 2 includes the ongoing activities. This is similar to any investment. For example, during Phase 1, when investing in stocks, you have to find a financial institution (such as Charles Schwab), open a brokerage account, and learn how to effectively invest in stocks. In Phase 2, you start buying and selling stocks, monitoring certain metrics, and making decisions to maximize your portfolio while minimizing risk.

So let's do just that for private lending.

Phase 1

In Phase 1, you set up the foundation to be able to start lending. Here are the non-recurring steps to building the foundation to being a private lender:

- Understand private lending, including pertinent laws and regulations
- Build your underwriting criteria, your policies, etc.
- Build your team
- Get the right training

Phase 2

In Phase 2, you start lending. Here are the recurring steps in being a private lender:

- Find borrowers
- Find sources for other people's money (OPM)
- Structure your deals for safety and profitability

Let's take a closer look at each of these.

Understanding Private Lending, Including Laws and Regulations

Lending is different in every state in the United States, and every country for that matter. So knowing your state's and country's lending laws and regulations is very important. For example, lending to owner-occupied borrowers (lending to people against the house they live in) is a lot more restrictive and regulated than lending to non-owner-occupied borrowers. The latter group is borrowing money to buy an investment property (that they don't live in) and is easier to lend to.

Furthermore, these laws and regulations change all the time. Having a team that understands all these laws and regulations is very important, and in fact, required.

But not to worry. There are people who specialize in dealing with all these laws and regulations. They specialize in handling these particular types of deals for private lenders and ensuring they comply with all pertinent regulations. They are licensed to do just that and can be found in most states. They are licensed mortgage brokers that focus on brokering private funds as opposed to institutional funds (like most mortgage brokers). They are known in the industry as "hard-money brokers" or "hard-money lenders." Most of them have a team of attorneys, title companies and appraisers that handle the majority of the work for them. Because of the negativity associated with the term "hard money," most simply refer to themselves as "private money lenders." They are licensed (in most states) to broker private funds.

However, individuals who want to become lenders are also known as private money lenders. So it's important to distinguish between a broker and the money person (us). Brokers often refer to us as "trust deed investors" or "private mortgage investors."

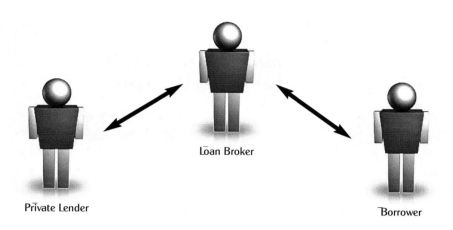

FIGURE 34: Always use a mortgage broker to do your real estate loans

DESCRIPTION	INDIVIDUAL	BROKER	BORROWER
Also known as…	• Private lender • Trust deed investor • Private mortgage investor	• Loan broker • Hard-money lender • Hard-money lender • Private lender	• Borrower • Investor • Property owner
How do they make money?	They make money through spreads, borrowing money at a lower rate and lending at a higher rate.	They make money primarily through charging points.	For investors, they make money borrowing the money to buy distressed properties and selling for higher value.
Notes	This is us.	These brokers are typically licensed.	

FIGURE 35: Comparison table of you (as lender), the broker, and the borrower

There are many differences. These brokers are, typically, licensed and we are not. They make their money by charging the borrower points. We make money on spreads. In more-advanced training, you'll learn about additional income streams, but for now, let's keep it simple.

For example, Yogesh is an engineer who works in the Silicon Valley. He met a hard-money broker named Rich, also a Californian. Rich makes money by finding and getting borrowers with their loan applications and all necessary documents to individuals, like Yogesh, who might be interested in their deal. For example, Rich found a client who wanted to borrow $200,000 against a property worth $350,000. Rich does the initial due diligence and thinks this is a good deal. He sends it over to Yogesh, and Yogesh does his own due diligence. Yogesh also likes the deal. So Yogesh agrees to fund it. Rich (the broker) and the borrower agree to the terms of the loan, as follows:

- 1-year loan
- 12% interest-only
- 5 points
- $200,000 loan amount

Yogesh funds the deal by sending the money directly to an escrow company. Five points of the loan amount, meaning 5% of the $200,000 (i.e., $10,000), go to the broker, Rich. The borrower gets the remaining money after paying other miscellaneous fees for the title and escrow. Now, the borrower starts making payments to Yogesh directly or through a servicing company (which is a company that accepts payments from the borrower for Yogesh). At the end of the first year, the borrower pays off the lender (Yogesh) the remaining balance of $200,000 and any remaining interest payments.

In this example, Rich is licensed to broker such loans, and Yogesh is a working professional who decides to do this to supplement his income. The confusion here is that the broker, Rich, calls himself a private money lender because of that negative connotation with the term "hard-money lender" we talked about. When Yogesh contacted Rich, he had to introduce himself as a trust deed investor; otherwise, if he had called himself a private lender, Rich would have thought that Yogesh was a competitor.

Building Your Underwriting Criteria, Policies, Risk Management, and More

Underwriting criteria are the conditions and standards or benchmarks you create that all your borrowers must meet and that will help minimize risk. These parameters are set by the lender (us) and are designed to filter the type of borrowers we are prepared to accept. For example, the parameters might include the types of properties you lend against (such as single-family residences and duplexes), the location of the property, whether it is owner-occupied or not, the credit requirements for the borrowers, the maximum loan to value (LTV), the down-payment requirements, the borrower's income, and more.

In addition to that, the policies document contains the rules you set for yourself. For example, always requesting an appraisal of the property could be included in your policies. Another policy could be that you always wire money to an escrow company and never to the borrower directly. Or you always get lender's title insurance (which the borrower pays for), and perhaps you should always be on the borrower's hazard insurance. Another could be that you never use the borrower's appraisal. The policies you establish should follow what are considered best practices in the industry.

The other document you need to consider having is a risk management table. This is typically a three-column document (in its simplest form) similar to the one shown below.

RISK	MITIGATION PLAN	CONTINGENCY PLAN
Risk description goes here	How to minimize or eliminate risk	What to do if risk does happen

FIGURE 36: Your risk, mitigation, and contingency plan worksheet outline

List all risks in the "Risk" column. Under "Mitigation Plan," list ways to minimize or eliminate that risk. In the "Contingency Plan" column, identify what to do if a "risk" becomes a "reality"!

RISK	MITIGATION PLAN	CONTINGENCY PLAN
Borrower stops paying	Low LTV. Make sure borrower has money into deal	Foreclosure. Call foreclosure company.
Property burns down	Make sure to be added as loss payee on borrower's insurance	Insurance company pays you as loss payee
Market drops fast (15%/year)	Low LTV (65%). Do short term loans (less than 1 year)	You still have enough protective equity with that drop. Still needs to pay you.

FIGURE 37: Your risk, mitigation, and contingency plan worksheet outline example

In the example shown, the risk is that the borrower stops paying you. The way to mitigate that risk is to make sure that you lend them a low LTV (perhaps 65% LTV) in the first place, which means the borrower has a lot of equity to lose. Also, make sure the borrower has money in the deal, which would make them think long and hard about walking away. The contingency plan is to call a foreclosure company and initiate foreclosure if that risk becomes reality.

Once you've created the first draft of these documents, you're ready to build your team. Team members will also help you update these documents.

Your team consists of:
- You
- Your mortgage broker (private money lenders or hard-money brokers), who specializes in brokering private funds
- Your bookkeeper
- Your accountant

Your mortgage broker obtains the remaining team members, including a real estate attorney that specializes in private lending, a servicing company (normally the broker), an appraiser, and others.

Finally, the right training will get you ready to excel in this arena without making too many costly mistakes; this is arguably the most important step in the whole process. As a private lender, you are the leader of your team. Not knowing how to play the game would be disastrous. For more information, refer to the Resource page in the back of this book.

Phase 2

In Phase 2 you begin lending, following the recurring steps to being a private lender.

First of all, finding borrowers is a lot easier than you think, and the process can even be automated. One such method is to have your mortgage broker or private money broker find you the borrowers and simply e-mail you the deals. You don't have to fund every deal, and in reality, you won't be able to fund most deals. Funding a couple of deals in the first few months is a good start.

Doing safer and more-profitable deals is about following your underwriting criteria and your policies, about structuring deals correctly, and about using strategies to enhance your profits.

The business will seem relatively simple once you've done a few deals. The broker sends you the loans, you compare to your underwriting criteria, you follow your policies to fund deals (if you choose to do them), and you structure the deals in a way that will be safer and most profitable for you. This whole process might take a total of 90 minutes or less – per loan! All of this starts with some education to help shape your success.

And the best part...the borrower pays for your whole team.

I recognized that I had disappointed Dr. Jazz by jumping to false conclusions. It should have been more obvious to me since banks have existed from the beginning of time for a reason. The business model works.

Dr. Jazz then said, "George, lending in every state is slightly different. That is an advantage in disguise. Only the ones committed to taking the time to learn are successful; the ones that expect everything handed to them on a silver platter will surely fail. I, personally, am glad that each state is a little different. It filters out 95% of the individuals not willing to spend a few weeks to learn their state requirements."

CHAPTER SUMMARY

- Becoming a private lender consists of two phases.
- Phase One: one-time setup of the foundation
  - Understand private lending, including pertinent laws and regulations
  - Build your underwriting criteria, your policies, etc.
  - Build your team
  - Get the right training
- Phase Two: ongoing activities
  - Find borrowers
  - Find sources for other people's money (OPM)
  - Structure your deals for safety and profitability

Refer to the Resources page for a free
bonus chapter with Dr. Jazz.

CHAPTER ELEVEN

The Banker's Rules

Dr. Jazz gently opened the manuscript to the page titled, "Banker's Rules."

"George, as you can see here, Herbert put together some assumptions. He called them 'rules.' He believed that for individuals using these financing strategies to succeed, these directives were critical; in fact, without them, he believed one would eventually fail."

"People have a tendency to make up their minds about something within the first few minutes of hearing about it. Do not do that here. Listen. Listen. Listen. You are being exposed to the greatest secrets on wealth building the world has ever known. But you must be patient and follow these rules," said Dr. Jazz sternly.

He paused to make sure I was paying attention, and there was a moment of silence as I let his message sink in.

"We've covered some of this already, but let's take the time for a little refresher course."

Every game has rules. Banking has its own rules.

The biggest challenge to becoming a successful private lender is the human factor, so we need the Banker's Rules, and we need to make sure that we follow the rules.

The difference between the Banker's Rules and all other rules is that almost all other rules are written by a third party to limit the benefits of the players in that game. For example, in the board game of *Monopoly*, the rules were written to limit the benefits of the players (investors). However, bankers wrote the Banker's Rules not to limit their benefits, but rather to maximize their own benefits, safely – an advantage and disadvantage at the same time. It is an advantage because you have the power to write your own rules and make money at it. And it is a disadvantage because there is no one to stop you from breaking your own rules, and that's a problem. That's when lenders start losing money.

Look at what happened to all the banks that started writing 100% LTV and 125% LTV loans. They got too greedy and broke their own rules, and rewrote new ones that shifted the risk to themselves. (In reality, they shifted the risk to the ultimate buyers of the notes – but that's a different story.)

So it's in your best interest to follow the rules you write to maximize wealth and to minimize risk and headaches! Heed them, and you prosper. Disregard them, and you pay the consequences.

Banking gives you a lot of power, but be careful. Power can backfire if you misuse it. So manage the power, but don't let it overpower you. Stay in control.

Rule No. 1: Banking is about safety. Shift the risk to the borrowers.

Read that again!

As a private lender, you learn to shift the risk to borrowers and take less risk when possible. Bankers make more money while taking on the safer position in a deal. Consider this. Many of the biggest buildings in cities across the globe have bank names plastered on the very top for a good reason – more profits with less risk. Lenders just do not like risk. They make money on the financing strategies of safer loans.

Never forget Rule no. 1!

Rule No. 2: Banking is about financing, not about investing.

We do not invest to make money; we make money by lending. It's a financing game.

You'll hear this statement: "We finance the risks of others." Consider this sentence for a moment. Simply put, it means that we finance our borrowers' risks by tying up all their collateral and taking on the more secure position. We do not absorb their risk. Investors (borrowers) are welcome to take as much risk as they like, but we want to be in a safer position. We do so by tying up any and all collateral we can get our hands on. We should have at least 150% of collateral tied up, as we shall find out later. That means for every $1,000 of money we lend, we need to tie up at least $1,500 of collateral.

Let me say it again: We finance; we do not invest.

Rule No. 3: Be a disciplined money manager.

Have control over spending habits. The power you get as a banker is the same power you can abuse. Because as a banker you have access to money, you can be tempted to spend it on items like a new car and new clothes. Always remember: You are not the consumer or the producer. In this equation you are the banker.

I'm not suggesting you shouldn't buy these things, but your "bank" should not buy them for you. Your bank should lend the money to you to buy them, and then you are obligated to pay back your own bank. I'll cover this in more detail in Chapter 12.

So, as a disciplined money manager (i.e., banker), you always want your money to be lent out, and you want to be receiving timely payments. Avoid the temptation to use the money for other activities or "toys."

Remember: Every dollar can either make you interest (work for you) or you can spend it and give up the interest you make on it. Said another way, the *real* cost of anything includes the interest you paid *and* the opportunity cost of not having that money working for you!

This is, by far, the biggest downfall of a banker. You've been warned.

Rule No. 4: Be an honest banker.

When you lend money to yourself to buy something, pay it back exactly the same way – at the same rate of interest – as if you had borrowed it from another lending institution! If you miss a payment back to your bank, make up that late payment as soon as possible!

This is a rule that bankers commonly break – because they have the power not to pay themselves. However, this is the first step to the demise of your bank! This rule cannot be overstated. You have to always pay back your bank.

Think of your bank as a separate entity. When you borrow money from it, treat it as you would any other lender or bank. Pay on time. If you're late, ask for an extension. Be "formal" with yourself.

Recognize that there are two sides to banking. You have the consumer on one side and the banker on the other. The consumer is the wealth spender. The banker is the wealth builder. We lend money to consumers to have them do all the work and pay us on time. We make the money. The minute we start thinking like a consumer, we lose the game. Act like a wealth builder (banker) and become an honest banker.

Rule No. 5: Remember The Golden Rule of banking: "Whoever has the gold makes the rules!"

Consumers do not save money. As a result, someone else must provide the capital necessary to sustain their way of life. This comes at a high cost. As a banker, with access to cash, you dictate the rules and the terms. In addition, all sorts of good opportunities will appear, and you can also negotiate favorable purchase prices.

So overcome the temptation to buy that new luxury car. Overcome the temptation to buy that mansion. Live within your means, and let your money work for you as you dictate the rules and the terms by which the borrowers buying these toys have to follow. They will make you wealthier while they work harder and harder.

Cash flow is everything! Access to capital is king. Control is everything.

Rule No. 6: Adopt the banker's habits.

Most people get into a comfort zone that causes them to lapse into their old way of doing things – a lifetime of conditioning that determines how one conducts oneself.

There's nothing worse than getting trapped in the comfort zone. Most people are stuck there and never get out. You must learn to develop new habits. Becoming a banker must become a way of life. You must use it or lose it! Ingrained habits are like muscle memory – you will have challenges in making these new habits work for you. Develop and adopt the banker's habits.

Rule No. 7: Follow the rules!

The biggest challenge to having a successful "banking system" is the human problem, so we need the Banker's Rules. And we need to make sure that we follow the rules.

The only thing holding anyone back from being able to develop this new banker mindset is overcoming human behavior. If you can control these, you can build wealth.

But if you break any rule, *you lose*!

"Doctor, these rules seem pretty straightforward," I said.

"Unfortunately, that's the downfall of most people that get involved in banking. The power of controlling money is a double-edged sword. It can make you wealthy, and it can also get you into trouble. It might seem easy now, but when you start controlling money, and especially lending it to yourself, you will understand," cautioned Dr. Jazz.

"If you break any rule, you lose! These rules are thousands of years old. They have been proven by the test of time! They have created dynasties!"

I nodded in agreement. I suddenly got a sense of the power of this secret. Banking has existed from the beginning of time. The wisdom of the ages was now being passed to me!

Little did I know that this information would eventually shape my life!

CHAPTER SUMMARY

- Every game has its rules. Banking has its own rules, too.

  Rule no. 1: Banking is about safety. Shift the risk to the borrowers

  Rule no. 2: Banking is about financing, not investing

  Rule no. 3: Be a disciplined money manager

  Rule no. 4: Be an honest banker

  Rule no. 5: The Golden Rule

  Rule no. 6: Adopt the banker's habits

  Rule no. 7: Follow the rules!

Refer to the Resources page for a free bonus chapter with Dr. Jazz.

CHAPTER TWELVE

Understanding the Banking System

ABOUT A WEEK LATER, DR. JAZZ ASKED ME TO MEET HIM AT A MEDICAL *office. I walked into the office in Danville, California, at exactly noon. It looked like a dentist's office – the posters on the walls of smiling people with dazzling, white teeth gave it away. I wasn't sure why I was there. Was Dr. Jazz hinting I needed some dental work?*

"Can I help you, sir?" asked the smiling woman behind the counter.

The only other person in the waiting room was a woman dressed in blue jeans and a ratty, gray t-shirt. Hunched down in a corner of the room, she looked in pain and kept her head bowed low, her hand on her cheek.

"Ummm. I…I…I was asked by Doctor Jazz to meet him here. Is there a Doctor Jazz here?" I asked. As I spoke, I realized that he might be a dentist here. I wasn't sure.

"Can I have your name, please?" she smiled with teeth that would get anyone to whiten theirs.

As I gave her my name, I saw Doctor Jazz walking out of an office with someone I assumed to be a patient.

"George, come in here," he beckoned. Another doctor walked into the waiting room and called the woman in the corner. She grimaced, and I hoped she soon felt better.

After the small talk, I asked Dr. Jazz, "Doctor, are you a dentist?"

"Yes, of course. I volunteer once a week with Doctor Jordan to help people who cannot afford a dentist. This used to be my practice, and we make sure we give back to the community. We do not turn down any patient," he said as he walked into an office.

"I asked you to come here so I could show you several things. First, I wanted to show you that private lending buys you the freedom of time to do what you want to do. I wanted to show you what I love to do. I love being a dentist and putting smiles on people's faces. That woman, for example, in the waiting room — she'll probably end up with some new teeth and a beautiful smile," he said.

"I also wanted to show you something else," he continued.

He pointed to the other rooms and all the big machines that looked like they were pieces of very expensive, state-of-the-art medical equipment.

"These machines cost me a lot of money. In fact, all the furniture, computers, medical equipment, monitors on the walls, and this whole office cost me a lot. I've been paying for this for years," he said.

I wasn't sure where he was going with this.

"Do you know how much money the 'bank' I borrowed the money from is making now?" he asked me. He had a cryptic smile on his face.

"A lot of money?" I replied.

"That's correct, George. Most other dentists borrow a lot of money to buy equipment like this. In fact, everyone borrows money from banks for all kinds of stuff," he says. "The reason I'm telling you this is that I borrowed the money from my own banking system, and I'm still paying the money back to my banking system. The money I borrowed to buy everything here alone has made me close to a million dollars over the many years!" he said. "Well, I should say 'my banking system' has made that much money," he corrected himself.

"Wow!" I was impressed.

"What exactly is a banking system and how does it work? And is this yours, as in, you own it?" I asked.

So far I've talked about lending other people money secured by their real estate. I explained how to lend out your (or other people's) money.

Now, let's turn the tables a bit. How about lending money to yourself?

Before I start providing details, I need to make this clear: All monies you lend to yourself must be your money and not other people's money. Let's start from the beginning.

> ## All monies you lend to yourself must be your money and not other people's money.

What is a Financing System?

Let's say you decide you want to buy a car. You walk into a dealership and pick the car you like, with the shiny rims and the best stereo system available.

There are three ways you can finance that purchase:
- Leasing
- Borrowing the money from a third-party lender, such as a bank or credit union
- Paying cash

FIGURE 38: Three ways to finance the new car

With all three of these methods, you lose money. When leasing and borrowing from a traditional bank, you lose money (interest) to the third-party source. In the third traditional way to purchase a car – paying cash – you lose your opportunity to use that money for investing in something or buying something else. This is called the "opportunity cost." So, in each of the traditional ways of buying/owning a car, you lose money each month to a third party, or you lose money you could have used in some other way.

PAYMENT METHOD	DESCRIPTION
Lease	Lose interest payments
Auto Loan	Lose interest payments
Cash	Now you have no money to invest, so you lose the opportunity to make money with that cash you used to buy the car

FIGURE 39: Three ways to finance the new car

A fourth method – another way of financing – is referred to as a "banking system." This requires a major shift in mindset. The problem most people have in understanding this is in trying to associate this fourth method with one of the other three traditional methods and not recognizing this as an alternative to the other three. Don't confuse this method with the others.

Assume you own a bank. Your bank lends you the money like any other bank. You buy the car, and you start making the loan payments to the bank. This is like any other loan; the difference now is that *you* own the bank. So essentially, you're taking money from one pocket to pay another. It's your bank, after all. Are you really losing this money? The answer is yes, partially, but the entity gaining the payments is your entity. So the money you would have paid another bank is now going into your bank.

Obviously, this bank does not exist. But anyone can use the concept of borrowing money from an entity they control to do this. It's not a true bank, but it serves like a privatized bank. Let's call this your "banking system."

- The banking system method allows you to recapture your interest.
- The other three methods — leasing, borrowing, or paying cash — cause you to lose money!
- With this new method, you build wealth!

By simply *using* this financing system, you're building wealth automatically. This will become more and more obvious as we go through this chapter. Follow along closely as I explain each step.

> ### The banking system method allows you to recapture your interest.
> ### By simply using your banking system, you're building wealth automatically.

Now, let's suppose you can buy some goods using your credit card. The credit card charges you 12% interest. Would you prefer to borrow money from your own banking system or from another bank? Obviously, if you're going to pay 12% anyway, why not pay it to your own banking system. After all, where else can you make an easy 12%? This is the same money you were going to pay to another bank regardless.

Let's revisit the car example. Instead of borrowing money from another bank to buy the car, you borrow it from your own banking system. If the auto loan was going to be 6% with the other bank, then you pay *your* banking system the 6%, not less. The cash you could have used in buying the car can now be used in possible investments, hopefully earning more than 6%.

FIGURE 40: Where is the average American income going to?

Let's suppose you get paid $5,000 per month. Believe it or not, 34.5% of the average American's income goes towards paying interest alone. This could include interest on mortgage payments, car payments, credit cards, etc. Assume in your case that $1,700 per month of your $5,000 goes towards paying interest alone. The average American saves very little at the end of the month, but let's suppose you're extremely diligent and that you save 5%. So, if you're lucky you're left with $250 in your pocket.

Recognize that, as you read this, that money is currently going out of your pocket to financial institutions.

The average individual is losing money every month in interest to third-party financial institutions! Utilizing a banking system allows you to recover at least some of that money. The cost of not doing this equals the monies paid and lost now and in the future for as long as you don't have a banking system in place.

Now, let's set up the banking system and see how things change. Remember that in our example you were paying $1,700 to third-party financial institutions. Let's replace these institutions with our own banking system. Also, assume you borrowed all the money from your own banking system, and now you're paying yourself back the $1,700. Your life has not changed. You're still paying the $1,700, but the recipient of that $1,700 changed. It's not the third-party financial institutions; it's your own banking system. Think of it as your other pocket.

Your personal life has not changed. You're still living the same lifestyle. You're not saving any less or any more. You're still getting $5,000 per month, still paying $1,700 per month in interest, still able to save $250 per month. The only thing that changed is that the $1,700 that's going out of your pocket has been "redirected" into your banking system, not to a third-party financial institution.

So by redirecting the interest payments into your financial institution – your banking system – you've recaptured these monies. You've borrowed money from your own banking system, and now you're just paying it back to yourself. Because you're paying yourself back, you're building up your own wealth by not paying for the same debt to an outside financial institution.

At this point you're probably thinking, "How do I get my banking system set up, and how does it lend me money? Where does my banking system get the money?" And a million other questions!

For most people, this is a foreign concept – difficult to accept and understand. For that reason, I'm going to be redundant in pressing the point home. I know that I'll be repeating the same concept and presenting it in different ways, and that's because I really want you to understand this before I go on. This is a foundational concept to the Financing System.

Up to now you had two choices when you purchased anything:
1. You could pay cash.
2. You could finance.

When you pay cash for something, in a sense you're still financing it, and this is where many people fail to understand the system. Every dollar you pay means you can't earn money elsewhere.

If you decide to pay cash for a car, you're still financing it, because you give up the opportunity to earn money elsewhere, which could prove more costly over time than actually financing the car with an auto loan.

What is the Significance of Having a Banking System?

Consider that 34.5% of the average American income goes towards paying interest alone. Over a lifetime, that will be a *lot* of money! If that money were placed in a tax-advantaged environment to grow at a good rate of return, the resulting amount of money could be significant.

Of course, there's no way you can redirect that money to your banking system overnight. However, as you start borrowing money from your banking system, you slowly start to divert some of that 34.5% back into it. And perhaps over the next six months, you might redirect 1% of the 34.5% into your system. Perhaps it could be as simple as borrowing money from your system to pay off your credit cards, and then start making monthly payments to your banking system with the same money you would have used to pay your credit card bills.

> **Your goal should be to redirect, as quickly as possible, most of that 34.5% into your banking system.**

Money Growth in Your Banking System

The money that resides in the banking system can grow in interesting ways.

1. It has to be growing in a tax-advantaged environment.

2. By using the power of velocity of money (described in Chapter 8), we start making money work for us and get higher returns.

3. We gain the opportunity to invest our personal cash (i.e., the cash we have, not cash already in the banking system) that we normally would have used to buy *stuff.* That cash can now be invested.

4. The money residing in the banking system should be earning money while sitting there (to be covered later).

5. Depending on the vehicle, you should be able to make a small spread on that money in the banking system (more to come, later).

Setting up Your Banking System

Like any small business, your banking system will need to be self-funded. Remember, it's your personal financing source. The money doesn't magically appear there. You have to fund it with your money.

So where does your money come from? There are several sources. Many people have money lying around earning next to nothing, such as a retirement account, savings accounts, CDs, stocks, bonds, etc.

"But I need to invest my money to make money!" you say. The obvious rejoinder is: Would you pay someone 6% when you're making only 1% on the same amount of money?

Take a look at this example.

Assume Bob (with the help of his wife, Julia) makes $100,000 in income per year. As an average American, $34,500 of that is going towards paying interest. Bob might save as much as $5,000 by the end of the year.

Most people end up placing that $5,000 in a savings account or CD at their local bank. Bob does the same and gets paid very little in interest. Meanwhile, Bob (like most people) is paying 10% or more on his other loans. So, instead of saving money or investing that $5,000, Bob can use it to "buy" some of the $34,500 – an income stream.

He does that by placing the $5,000 in his banking system, then using part of that to pay off existing loans, which effectively transfers the loan from a third-party financial institution to his banking system. Bob continues to make payments on the loans, but the payments – part of his $34,500 worth of interest payments – are now going into his banking system. It's important to recognize that Bob is *not* paying off his loan with that $5,000; he's essentially having his banking system *buy* the loan from the other financial institution while continuing to receive the payments from the borrower (himself).

Now, instead of earning a small return from a CD or savings account, Bob's banking system is earning the same interest rate he was paying the other financial institution! If he had been paying 8% on the loan, then Bob's banking system would receive that 8%.

So, here's what happens (refer to the three diagrams below). A portion of that $34,500 in interest paid per year will start getting redirected to Bob's banking system. Notice how, over time, the amount going to the Third-Party Lender gets lower as the amount going to Bob's banking system gets higher.

**FIGURE 41: 1st Day of your banking system.
34.5% still going to traditional bank**

**FIGURE 42: End of 1st year of your banking system (example).
A potion has been redirected to your banking system**

**FIGURE 43: End of 2nd year of your banking system (example).
A bigger portion has been redirected to your banking system**

What Vehicle Should One Use for Their Banking System?

The vehicle (refer to Chapter 9) has to have certain characteristics, the most important of which is the tax-advantaged environment. Let me expand on that again. You can run your banking system from a tin can, a checking account, or any one of many vehicles. However, it turns out that one of the ideal vehicles is permanent insurance. Now, we've been conditioned to stay away from certain life insurance; however, this is very different.

With *permanent* insurance, you have basically two options: Whole Life and Universal Life. Both of these have two components, called the "death benefit" and the "cash value (or "cash surrender value"). You can think of the death benefit as going towards maximizing your death pay-out when you die. Think of the cash value as somewhat like a savings account. When you buy permanent insurance, the life insurance agent sets it up so that most of the money you pay goes towards the death benefit and less to the cash value.

Permanent Insurance

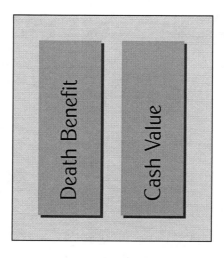

FIGURE 44: Two pieces of permanent insurance

The "typical" setup is to maximize the death benefit and minimize the cash value. However, for our banking system, we want it the other way around. We like the characteristics of the cash value, which would work ideally for our banking system. So we actually want to maximize the amount of money in the cash value and minimize the death benefit.

The diagram below shows the allocated percentage of the premium payment. In the "typical" setup, a higher percentage of the payment goes towards the death benefit and a smaller percentage towards the cash value. With the banking system, it's the other way. A higher percentage of the premium payment goes towards the cash value and a smaller percentage towards the death benefit.

"Typical" Setup   "Banking System" Setup

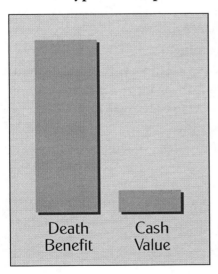
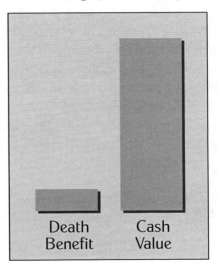

FIGURE 45: Comparison of typical insurance setup and banking system. The bars represent the allocation % of payments

The problem is that most insurance agents are not familiar with how to set up everything correctly; there's a lot to know and a lot more to it. Make sure you find a competent insurance agent who can support your plans correctly. For a list of potential insurance agents, please refer to the Resources page at the back of this book.

> ## Find the right insurance agent to set up your insurance for you.
> ## The wrong agent can cost you a lot!

When you've set up the insurance policy, you fund it with the intention of the money going towards the cash value. Once there, you can start using it as a banking system. Let's say that you now have $50,000 in your banking system. That $50,000 will be earning a decent return. As an example, let's say your money is earning 6%.

When you decide to borrow some of that money, you actually don't borrow *your* money; the insurance company lends you *their* money that is secured by your money. So if you decide to borrow $10,000, they'll lend you that money at some interest rate, say 5% for this example. Your $50,000 is still sitting in the cash-value account earning 6% (in this example).

"Banking System" Setup

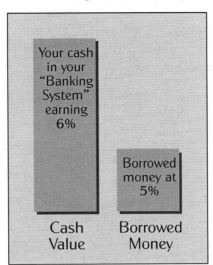

**FIGURE 46: Borrowed money from banking system
is secured by your money (the cash value)**

In this example, you're paying 5% on money earning 6%, giving you a spread of 1%. You lend that money to yourself at 10%. Instead of paying another financial institution, you now pay your own banking system the 10%.

Let's look at what's going on in your banking system now. In this example, the money residing there is growing at 6%, and it's receiving 10% from you as a borrower, and that borrowed money is costing 5%. So all in all, the banking system is getting 10% + 6% − 5% = 11%. That money is growing at 11% in a tax-advantaged environment − in addition to getting the bonus of a death benefit, just in case!

"Banking System" Setup

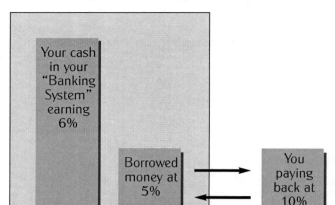

**FIGURE 47: Borrowed money from banking system
is secured by your money. The columns represent total amounts (dollars)**

Where else can you get 11% like this, knowing it's growing in a tax-advantaged environment? I can almost hear some people saying, "But who would pay 10% and why?" Open your credit card statement right now! Seriously, go ahead and open it. Most people are paying at least 10% to other financial institutions. Some are paying 12%, 18%, 24%, even as much as 30%! All we're doing is redirecting these payments to your own banking system. Think of the banking system as doing a deal with yourself. It says to you, "We will pay off your credit card, but we ask that you pay us whatever you were paying them." If you're wondering why you would pay your own banking system the same interest rate, it's simple. You have to start thinking like a banker. Stop thinking like a consumer! Run your banking system like its own "bank."

If you thought the 11% from the above example was exciting, once you start using velocity of money, your banking system will start increasing its internal rate of return. All of that is more money in your banking system.

For more information, refer to the Resources page in the back of the book.

Review

Assume that your income is $100,000 per year. Now, consider the following question:

How much would you pay to receive an income stream of $34,500 of interest per year for the rest of your life?

That's how much the lending institutions are getting every year in interest – from your pockets (on average) – if you're making $100,000 a year. The banking system allows you to recapture that income stream leaving your pocket today and redirect it into your own banking system.

If you're able to save $5,000 per year, don't think, "What interest rate can I get on my $5,000 savings?" Instead, think, "I need to use this $5,000 to *recapture* some of that $34,500 in interest I pay every year!"

First, you get your permanent life insurance policy as a banking system. You fund it with your own money that's lying around doing very little. You start lending yourself money for purchases you normally make and pay back your banking system, with interest, just as you would any other financial institution. Over time, you start paying less and less to third-party financial institutions and more and more to your banking system.

Warning!

Your own banking system is a great way to build wealth. However, be aware that getting this structured correctly is very important. Also, be aware of the importance of the insurance agent you select. I've not had good experience with insurance agents. Many of them seem honest enough, but I still have had bad experiences. I can't warn you enough against working with the wrong individual. Many agents position themselves as experts with banking systems, but please be careful. For example, I worked with a couple of men from Utah that presented themselves as experts with banking systems. Unfortunately, they proved to be dishonest and the worst kind of individuals anyone could work with. Please, do your due diligence.

Some "experts" are extreme advocates of using the banking system for any and every loan. I disagree. For example, if you can get an auto loan for 0% to buy a car, why would you use your banking system to do that? Use the third-party financial institution. Some of these "experts" insist on using your banking system to buy the car loan and charging yourself a higher interest! They're not considering the opportunity cost. Just use common sense and ask a lot of questions!

Your banking system can truly be a great wealth builder. Use it.

Frequently Asked Questions

Q: By being a banker, is Bob keeping more money in his pocket at the end of the month?

A: Not necessarily. The same amount of money is going out each month, but if Bob is clever and is allowing that money to stay in his banking system, he doesn't necessarily have more buying power *now*. He needs to think of the banking system as a separate entity, even though in truth, his money is leaving one pocket and entering another. His banking system is building wealth, but not for himself. At the end of it all, Bob owns the banking system.

Q: By being a banker (in this context alone), is Bob "bleeding" less money every month?

A: No, he's living the same lifestyle with the same amount of cash available to him.

Q: By being a banker, is Bob and his banking system one and the same?

A: Although this question is subjective, the best answer is that Bob and his banking system are two different entities. Bob is an individual, and his banking system is a separate entity.

Q: Is Bob's lifestyle any different (in the context of this chapter)?

A: The only thing that has changed is that Bob can borrow money from his banking system more easily because they already have a relationship.

Q: What has changed since Bob started his banking system?

A: The only thing that has changed is that Bob is borrowing from his banking system rather than from another bank or credit card lender.

"Doctor, that's amazing! How much can one make in having their own banking system?" I asked excitedly.

"Well, it depends on many factors: age, health, how often you borrow the money, among other things. But here are some things to think about. If you do this right, at your age…George, I can see you making seven figures! And keep in mind, this is the same money that you're already paying to third-party lenders. We are not talking about going out and investing. We are simply talking about money that is leaving your pocket as we speak," he said as he pointed to my pocket with a smile.

I was blown away by this.

"So, can we use the banking system to lend money out to other people, like you talked about before?" I asked.

"Absolutely. The key to remember is that you want to place your own money in the banking system, not borrowed money. When you end up lending money to yourself, it comes from your banking system. When you lend money to others, it could come from one of three sources: your banking system, your personal cash (not in the banking system), and other people's money."

I was starting to get it.

CHAPTER SUMMARY

- At the basic level, the banking system will recapture all of your interest payments! You then grow your money in your "bank" using velocity and compounding in a tax-advantaged environment.
- Banking system is a method of finance.
- Traditional financing methods are:

    Leasing

    Borrowing

    Paying Cash

- Banking system is a fourth method.
- In the first three methods, you either lose money to the finance source, *or* you lose the opportunity cost.

Refer to the Resources page for a free
bonus chapter with Dr. Jazz.

CHAPTER THIRTEEN

Let's Combine Everything

"So, Dr. Jazz, I see how powerful being the bank is. So are you saying you're a banker? Or do you own a bank? Or for that matter, are you a full-time lender?"

"No, George," he laughed. "Let me ask you this. What are your dreams in life?"

"Well. I have many, but the big one is this. A hundred years from now, no one will know who most of the people that are alive today are. Go to the cemetery and you see names from the past, most of them unknown to anyone but family. But they all have their stories; they all came and went. I want to enjoy the journey, and most important, I want to leave something that makes this world a little bit better because of my contribution. I wish I could find a cure for cancer. I wish I could make every child happy. For me, if someone a hundred years from now could say that I helped in some way, I'd feel like I had made a difference, especially with my family and generations to come. I want to help, in my own way, open people's eyes, help them to live a better life. I want to help them understand this amazing information, help educate them with all of this so they can have a better life. It's really that simple," I laughed as I took a breath.

"But tell me, what are your dreams?" I asked Dr. Jazz as I tried to change the subject.

"George, those are great goals!" he said as he paused for a few seconds. He was transfixed in thought, like he was analyzing what I had just said.

"Well, George, going back to your question about me owning a bank or being a full-time lender, here is what you need to know. Life is more than just money. It's about enjoying an incredible journey through life. It's about giving back, learning, and enjoying it. The income from lending buys me the time to do so. It buys me freedom of time to do whatever I want in my life. I know that some people to whom I've passed this information used their time to become teachers, to build businesses, or to run charities. When you have enough money to live on, then you need to live! You need to recognize that life is not about being a lender or being a business person, life is about the journey.

"So, to answer your question, I'm not a banker or a full-time private lender. I do not own banks, either. I simply make money like a bank. I use the same strategies to generate passive income while I give back to the world in my own way," he said with a smile, waiting for a reaction from me.

"How do you do that? How do you give back?" I questioned.

He laughed.

Let's look at a typical day in the life of an established private lender. Stella wakes up in the morning, excited about the possibilities. As a single mom, she's grateful she gets to fix breakfast for her two children and then take them to school herself – unlike the other single moms she knows.

She pours herself some tea and walks over to her laptop on the coffee table where she left it the night before. She checks her e-mail and reads a message from her broker about a loan request from a potential borrower. It looks like a good deal, and this same property buyer had borrowed private money from her in the past. He purchased a $200,000 home less than 30 minutes from her house for $150,000, and she had lent him $120,000 (60% LTV) for 12%. She borrowed the money at 6%, and within eight months he had paid her back.

She reviews the new loan request form filled out by her broker. He's already reviewed the loan and given his initial blessing, so she decides to do the loan. She replies to the e-mail and informs her broker she's in for 50% of the loan request. She understands that it's better to distribute her risk. To minimize the risk, her goal is to have a greater number of smaller, rather than larger, loans. She's taken the time to educate herself about private lending, thinking like a lender and minimizing risk.

She takes a break and gets some exercise with a brisk walk around the neighborhood, stopping to chat with her elderly neighbor next door. She goes to her workshop in the backyard when she gets home and works on her latest stained-glass project.

After an hour or so, Stella goes back inside to check out the news on the Internet. She logs into her bank account and notices two smaller deposits – one for $82 and another for $352 – that had gone straight to her line of credit. She knows the money came from two of the many loans she has, and smiles, knowing what little work she had to do for that money. She recognizes that as soon as this money comes in, she needs to lend it back out. It is, after all, about keeping the money moving.

She had automated the task of finding borrowers, no longer having to market for them. Her broker was sending her more than enough! She had also automated the task of doing safer loans and implemented several layers to minimize her risk. With the help of her broker, she had developed her underwriting criteria and strictly followed them. She made sure all her deals went through a qualified broker that understood the process of qualifying loans and shifting risks away from the lender. And she always made sure the loan transactions and money went directly through the local title company. She had built a great team and was educated about the business.

She calls her friend, Sylvia, and they chat for awhile, agreeing to meet for lunch at one of their favorite sushi restaurants. Sylvia is another private lender, and they take their time catching up, sympathizing about the usual family nonsense, and discussing the deals they're doing and additional opportunities they're working on. They walk next door, and over their favorite ice cream, they continue to plan their upcoming trip to Italy. Sylvia is helping Stella learn Italian, and they laugh frequently at her expense.

Stella pays for their lunch with a card that's paid for by her own, private banking system. She knows everybody spends money on "liabilities," but as long as her banking system is financing it all, she'll gladly pay it back with interest, making her system rich without changing her spending.

They drive around the block to shop in the neighborhood mall and bump into an old school friend of theirs, Kelly, laden with shopping bags from a number of stores. Back in the day, Kelly was the all-American girl, a cheerleader, part of the popular crowd – you get the idea. Today it sure looked like she was a shopaholic. Kelly had always lived extravagantly, and by all appearances, most would think she was rich. Stella and Sylvia hope their pity doesn't show on their faces; Kelly doesn't know that her husband has called both of them requesting a loan, and they realize that Kelly and her husband are living a lie. They live paycheck to paycheck, have $67,000 of credit card debt, and are barely making it. They're the ideal consumers who work hard and send their money to producers and lenders. Stella and Sylvia say hello, spend a few minutes talking to Kelly, and continue with their shopping.

Mid-afternoon, Stella receives a text message on her cell phone, a timely reminder from her debt management software to pay particular bills. She has her finances automated, where bills are paid with a click of a button. Her debt management software lets her know the ideal time to pay specific bills, and she can be anywhere in the world to do that. She makes a mental note to pay her bills when she gets back home.

On her way home, she decides to pass by one of the properties she had lent money against. It's in a nice, upper-middle-class neighborhood. The owner (and borrower) is an executive in a high-tech company. She notices as she drives by that all the lights are off in the house, and the husband and wife are both still at work. They work long hours at demanding jobs while their kids are with babysitters to pay for all the debts the parents have incurred. Stella congratulates herself for taking the time to educate herself, to adopt the banker's mindset, and to create the life she always dreamed of. She was setting the rules for the game most others were playing, the ones stuck in the consumer trap. She understood that being on the earning side of interest, especially compound interest, was the best place to be. She decides to take the kids out to their favorite restaurant to celebrate when she gets home.

Later that evening over a glass of wine by the fire, Stella logs into her automated bill-paying website. She sees that she has to pay several bills. She pays them from her "wealth account" (her line of credit), knowing that paying from that account is allowing her to make her money work for her. She was tired of working hard for her money and now realizes how amazing it is having her money do the hard work instead. She also recognizes that her "wealth account" is allowing her to pay off her debts *fast*!

Having quickly taken care of business, she spends time with her children, helping them with their homework and playing a game of *Scrabble*. They talk excitedly about the trip to Disneyland they're planning with their cousins and her sister, and Stella knows she'll need to borrow money for the trip. Her sister will also need to borrow money on her credit card, but her cards are "maxed out," so she'll have to call the credit card company and request an increase in her limit.

Stella knows the lender *she's* borrowing money from – herself – the one she sees everyday in the mirror. She decides to lend herself the money from her banking system and quickly prints a promissory note for the amount, signs it, and files it. She also prints a loan repayment worksheet and coupon book.

She knows her money is growing in a tax-advantaged environment. She has liquidity and controls her own "economy." She's not dependent on the "real" economy like her sister, whose request for a credit increase might be denied because of that same economy. Only Stella can deny her own request; she is, after all, the banker.

After the kids had been read to and were in bed, Stella's friend, Nate, arrives in her driveway with a brand new Jaguar. The car looks stunning, and Stella tells Nate exactly that. He's very proud of the beautiful leather interior and sunroof, and he has more features to show her. She knows, though, that Nate has a consumer's mindset. He has to work harder now as an engineer to make up for the higher car payments.

Stella would never buy a car like that by financing it with a third-party lender. If her bank could finance it, and she had enough money coming in from her borrowers every month, she might then consider it.

Stella smiles and congratulates Nate, truly happy for him. She knows that, unlike Nate, her mindset has shifted over the years from the consumer's to the banker's mindset, recognizing immediately how easy it would be to shift back to that consumer's mindset like Nate.

After another amazing day spent with loved ones and good friends, great food and leisurely fun, Stella goes straight to bed and rests stress-free. Stella understands that her borrowers are paying for her lifestyle. She also made a commitment to herself that anytime she wanted to buy "toys" (cars, vacation homes, high tech devices), she would have to lend herself more money and have the borrowers' interest payments pay for the bills.

Let's look at Stella's portfolio.

- Her money is growing exponentially in a tax-advantaged environment. It's also beating inflation.

- Being the banker allows Stella to generate passive income and some level of liquidity.

- She owns her primary residence, along with two rental properties within a 30-minute drive. Both rental properties were paid off from private money-lending payments and have a 70% LTV HELOC (home equity line of credit) that Stella uses to lend even more. The rent coming in is $2,300 per month.

- In addition to the two rental properties, Stella has bought two more rental properties using a strategy (taught by her mentor) on minimizing the risk of rental properties. The strategy involves spreading the risk among two or more investors. Given that they thought like bankers and understood how to minimize risk, Stella and the other investor had purchased these properties as tenants-in-common and had agreed to pay down the mortgage. They had put no money down and, to pay down the mortgage, they were using private lending money.

- What does her "savings account" look like? One of the things that stands out is how the banker's account is different from that of someone who is "saving" money. This is not a "forced" savings account. Let's compare them.

SAVER	BANKER
Mindset: I need to "save" money and live below my means	Mindset: I need to "lend" money to live well
Dead money	Moving money
Bank account balance is higher	Bank account balance is lower due to money being "moving" and not static
Making money on interest from bank	Making money from lending money
Lending money to bank	Borrowing money from "saver"
Money losing buying power due to inflation	Money gaining buying power due to returns beating inflation
Works hard for their money	Makes money work hard for them
No income stream	Consistent cash flow coming in
Loss of a job can be devastating to savings due to lack of income stream	Loss of job does not have a devastating effect due to cash flow
I can afford to retire when I have saved enough money	I can afford to retire when I have enough cash flow to pay my bills
"At retirement, I have to make sure I do not live beyond my savings"	"At retirement, I have enough income for as long as I live"
Pays down their mortgage to feel safer – but actually making lender safer and their equity riskier	Uses the equity to generate cash flow and has borrowers pay down mortgages

FIGURE 48: The consumer's mindset versus the banker's mindset

- And maybe best of all: Stella has more time – and money – to do what she enjoys.

"Why would you do anything else when you know you can make more money, take the safer position in a deal, and have someone else do all the work while they take on the riskier position?" asked Dr. Jazz.

"George, banking is the greatest wealth-building strategy ever invented," said Dr. Jazz confidently.

"Enjoy life, George. You never know when your time is up," he said. "You should look back on your life and say, 'I lived it!'"

"The truth is, George, it's never about the money. It's about the life."

CHAPTER SUMMARY

- Over time, private lenders start thinking very differently from consumers or savers.

Refer to the Resources page for a free bonus chapter with Dr. Jazz.

CHAPTER FOURTEEN

"I Want To Be A Real Estate Investor"

I CALLED DR. JAZZ FOUR DAYS LATER. IT WAS ABOUT 10:17 A.M. PACIFIC TIME.

"Good morning, Dr. Jazz. Is this a good time?" I asked.

"Good morning, George. How are you doing today?"

Dr. Jazz was a very proper man, particular about many things. I had learned a lot about him in the short time I knew him. He always wore a suit with a hat. He always walked everywhere. He always spoke properly. He insisted on sitting properly and wanted everybody else to sit properly, too. Shoes must be on the floor, soles down. He had, on a number of occasions, asked me not to put one foot over the other.

"I'm doing great, Doctor, thank you. I have a favor to ask. I'm sitting with a friend of mine, and I was sharing with her what you told me about lending. But she insists she wants to be a real estate investor. I was wondering if you could help me change her mind, please? Her name is Cara," I said as I switched to speaker phone.

"Good morning, Dr. Jazz. My name is Cara, and I've heard a lot about you. George has shared so much information with me about being a private lender, I can tell he's been transformed. But, I'm not convinced, and I was wondering why you would argue against being a real estate investor instead?"

139

"Good to talk with you, Cara. If you want to be a real estate investor, then I think you should be a real estate investor. I'm a big advocate of real estate investors. I never said not to be one, George," he chided me.

"I thought you told me that being a private lender is the best wealth strategy there is," I stammered.

"George, what would happen if everyone out there were a lender? You'd have no borrowers, and no one would make money. You need to balance the ratio of lenders to borrowers to consumers. Without that, you'd have a problem. So, by all means, you should encourage Cara to be a real estate investor. They, too, offer value to renters and other homeowners, and they profit from it. In fact, real estate is one of the most important drivers for economies, and we all need each other. This is a win-win-win situation," he concluded.

Private lenders need real estate investors, and real estate investors need consumers who are looking for rental properties or homes to buy. They also need private lenders. Real estate brokers, appraisers, title companies, attorneys, insurance companies, and many others businesses benefit from real estate transactions.

Real estate can be a very profitable business; however, mastering real estate investing is critical to success.

Understanding the differences between a private lender and a real estate investor can be helpful. Let's take a look.

Real estate investing has four profit centers:
- Cash flow

- Appreciation

- Paying down of the mortgage

- Tax benefits

Most investors rank cash flow as the number one reason they buy real estate, followed by appreciation.

Let's focus on cash flow first.

Income property is a property purchased for the purpose of generating income by renting out units. You can have commercial tenants or individual consumers. A good income property deal that is performing will pay approximately 12% cash-on-cash return. That's a good-performing deal and does not include a distressed property that needs major rehabilitation. With private lending, you can make the 12% cash-on-cash return relatively easily. You don't have to look too far. But let's keep going.

The down-payment on an income property is the highest risk position in which to put either your money or the money you raised. Would you truly take $1,000,000 of your cash and put it in a riskier position to make $10,000 per month, knowing that it is in the riskiest position in real estate? Even worse, would you put other people's money in the riskiest position, knowing that they will make, perhaps, $5,000 per month?

What if you could place your money, or the money raised, in a safer position, and then pay your private lender more?

So far, we've discussed returns and risk. We said that the returns between private lending and income properties are the same. In fact, private lending can bring much better returns. As far as the risk of the money is concerned, private lending can be a much safer position than ownership of the income property.

Now let's look at liquidity.

When you use your money (or other people's money) as a down payment on a performing property, the money is locked up in that property for years, typically a minimum of five or more. However, with private lending, the commitment can be for a shorter term and is, therefore, relatively liquid. But, you can also borrow against it. Another instance of hypothecation. You can pledge your note as collateral and borrow against it. This makes the note much more liquid than a down payment.

As you can see, in all three areas – liquidity, returns, and safety –private lending is better.

However, this is not to say that private lending is better than owning properties. It turns out that a combination of both is ideal. Owning properties has many advantages. In fact, property ownership, if done right, is still one of the best wealth-builders. Combining both private lending for cash flow and property ownership for the four profit centers (listed above) is a better portfolio than private lending alone.

In fact, one of the advanced strategies combines private lending with property ownership, where the private-lending payments pay off the mortgages on the properties relatively quickly. And as properties get paid, the equity is turned to HELOC (home equity lines of credit) as a money source for more private lending. It's not uncommon for advanced private lenders to own several homes, all paid off by borrowers from the private money loans.

The key point to remember is that private lending is the most efficient passive-income strategy in existence. By combining it with other strategies, you start gaining the advantages of other investment vehicles.

Which of the next scenarios would you prefer to have?

- Owning several rental properties, knowing that you might have a few bad months and that you may be required to provide additional capital (which you do not have).

- Or, have passive income coming in first, and then purchase some rental properties, knowing that if you ever have a few bad months, you can cover them with the passive income.

Which would you prefer? It's really that simple.

As I hung up the phone, Cara turned to me with a look on her face like a deer caught in the headlights. Her mind was spinning. She could say only one word:
"Wow!"

CHAPTER SUMMARY

- Private lenders and real estate investors need each other.
- In terms of returns and cash flow, income properties and private lending are similar. In fact, private lending can be more profitable.
- In terms of safety, private lending is safer than property ownership.
- In terms of liquidity, private lending can be more liquid than the down-payment for property ownership.
- A combination of private lending and owning properties is ideal.
- Advanced private lenders often own several homes, all paid off by borrowers from the private-money loans.

Refer to the Resources page for a free bonus chapter with Dr. Jazz.

CHAPTER FIFTEEN

"I Want To Invest in the Stock Market"

THREE DAYS LATER, AS I WAS DRIVING DOWN THE FREEWAY TO SAN RAMON, I decided to ask Doctor Jazz about the stock market. My wife and many others believed the stock market to be a safe, investment vehicle.

"Doctor Jazz, I was talking to my wife about the banking concepts you shared with me. I'm truly blown away by them, but my wife feels we should stick to the stock market. What do you think of that?" I asked.

"George, you can do whatever you want. I never give financial advice to anyone; I simply share my knowledge and experience. Investing in the stock market works well for some people. But would you like my personal opinion on the matter?" he asked.

"Sure. ... Please tell me."

"Well, it's not going to be good. But here goes."

The stock market is an interesting vehicle, but it's probably not exactly what you think it is.

The Stock Market as a Zero-Sum Game

Do you believe playing poker is investing? If you said "no," then let me ask you this: Isn't someone at the table making money by investing a certain amount of money and enjoying returns after playing the game? Doesn't that sound like the stock market "game"?

Nevertheless, poker is *not* investing; it's a zero-sum game.

Consider a quote from the main character, Gordon Gecko, of the 1987 movie, *Wall Street*: "It's not a question of enough, pal. It's a zero-sum game; somebody wins and somebody loses. Money itself isn't lost or made; it's simply transferred from one perception to another." He was talking about the stock market!

Let's imagine a poker game with three players. Each player has 10 chips (30 chips total). By the end of the game, one player ends up with 0 chips, another player has 28 chips, and the third player has 2 chips. There are still only 30 chips in the game. No chips appeared or disappeared. The chips were simply transferred from one player to another. For the winner to win, someone else had to lose. All of the chips that came into the game left the game. This is called a "zero-sum game."

The NASDAQ glossary gives the following definition of a Zero-Sum Game:

> A situation in which one participant's gains result only from another participant's equivalent losses. The net change in total wealth among participants is zero; the wealth is just shifted from one to another.

Examples of zero-sum games include checkers, poker, and gambling, in general. Another example of a zero-sum game is a Ponzi Scheme. In a Ponzi Scheme, each "player" pays a fixed amount to the player who recruits him. This new player then goes out and recruits more players, and thus profits from their buy-in payment. Every dollar that the early players take away from the scheme is paid into the scheme by some other player. Who are the losers? The last people to enter the game –

when there are no more people to recruit – lose their entry fee. Meanwhile, their losses exactly match the profits of the early adopters.

It turns out that the stock market is a zero-sum game, too. Every dollar that some investor "wins" in a stock market investment, some other investor lost. As Gecko observes in *Wall Street*, money in the stock market is *shifted* from one person to another. No wealth is created; it's simply shifted.

Unlike in poker, however, people investing in the stock market can't tell if they're winning or losing (except for brokerage fees, which are pure losses) until they cash out. The stock brokerage fees make the sum non-zero (negative). Many people argue that the stock market is not a zero-sum game; they want you to believe the sum is positive, but those brokerage fees actually make it worse than zero. The broker is like the house in a casino, and the house always wins.

It's possible to argue that certain stocks pay dividends, making the stock market a positive sum game (a profit). I'm not including this strategy in this discussion. Most people buy stock for trading; i.e., buy low, pray it goes up, and sell. I'm also excluding dividend investors, focusing instead on the investors seeking profits from capital gains.

There are many commonly believed *wrong* assumptions about the stock market. Let's look at a few.

The Stock Market Creates Wealth

No dollar ever comes out of the market into an investor's pocket that didn't first get into the market from some other investor's pocket. (Once again, in this case I'm excluding investors investing for dividends.) The underlying companies whose stock is being traded can create wealth, but none of that wealth ever shows up in the stock market — unless the company buys back its own stock and goes private. All transactions just move money from one investor to another. No wealth is created or destroyed in the process, except for the brokerage fees. Money is simply transferred. So the stock market does not create wealth; it simply shifts wealth.

Total Market Capitalization Increases

This has nothing to do with whether or not the market is a zero-sum game. Imagine twenty games of poker, with four to six players in each game, and all the money adding up to one million dollars. Now, imagine that the games were augmented with an additional sum of two hundred thousand dollars, bringing the total of all money in the games to one million, two hundred thousand dollars. Does it mean poker is not a zero-sum game?

This same argument applies to the stock market. More people joining the game or adding more money to the game doesn't make the stock market a positive-sum game. Each company is still a zero-sum game, and the sum of many zero-sum games is still zero. The size of the pot on the table during one hand is irrelevant to the question of whether the winnings of the winners equal the losses of the losers.

This Magazine (or Book) Said the Stock Market is a Good Place to Invest

Who are the advertisers in the magazine? Do you think they'd pay to advertise if the magazine promoted information contrary to their interests? What companies are behind the publishers of that magazine? It's probably some financial institution. What about all those books? Who are the publishers? My first book on investing was called, *Guide to Understanding of Money and Investing* and was published by *The Wall Street Journal!* It should be no surprise what *The Wall Street Journal* wants to promote.

To sum up, you're not *investing* in the stock market, you're *speculating*. The investment community has long used smoke and mirrors to make you think you're investing.

Professor Lawrence Harris, chairman of the Department of Finance at the University of Southern California, and chief economist of the

Securities and Exchange Commission (SEC), explains it best in his paper, "The Winners and Losers of the Zero-Sum Game."

Professor Harris provides an unbiased opinion about the losers. He admits they are necessary for the market to function efficiently; the market will not function efficiently without the typical buy-and-hold stock investor!

Another good read on this topic is the book, *Trading for a Living*, by Dr. Alexander Elder, considered the "bible" of trading. The author shares his experience as a professional trader and claims that markets are created for most traders to lose money. He says, "The trading industry keeps draining huge amounts of money from the markets.... Markets need a fresh supply of losers.... Losers bring money into the markets, which are necessary for the prosperity of the trading industry." Dr. Elder calls the stock market a "minus-sum game," where winners gain less than losers lose because the industry takes money from the market to pay the fees for dealers and brokers. Dr. Elder thinks that being better than average is not enough; you need to be better than the crowd playing on the stock market to win a minus-sum game.

Now that you know you're essentially playing poker with other players, ask yourself this: Against whom are you playing? Many investors simply buy and hold stocks, while the financial institutions hire the best full-time traders to compete against them. Even more disturbing is the fact that institutions are automating the trading with computers using very sophisticated algorithms that trade super-fast. So the average investor is now competing with computers, along with some of the best stock traders in the world!

Am I suggesting not investing in the stock market? No, but I am suggesting that you need to open your eyes and be aware of the reality. We are constantly bombarded by financial institutions encouraging us to invest their way – we assume the risk and they make the money. This type of investing has become conventional wisdom, because the financial institutions have done a great job of "educating" us through their sponsored magazines, books, and television programs.

Stock Market Lies

We just exposed the stock market as a minus-sum game, essentially a big casino. It gets worse when we look at the numbers we're being fed by the stock brokers.

"Don't believe everything you hear or see." True for politics, but also for the financial sector. The fact is, when it comes to power and money, it's best to keep a healthy distrust of "specialists." They all make money from our mistakes, aware that the average individual without the right specialized knowledge can't verify what they sell as the unqualified truth.

Let's consider this financial "fact" (using the word loosely): "Statistically, the stock market provides a consistent profit of 10.4 percent." In fact, it doesn't, even if you hope to invest for 76 years in the stock market index, the only assumption under which this return is mathematically possible. It's become the norm for potential profits to be exaggerated (a lot), when typically we don't see any profits at all.

For example, let's say I invest $20,000 in a mutual fund that has an estimated 10 percent return. In the first year, I enjoy a 100 percent positive rate of return, so I have $40,000 in my brokerage account. In the second year, the market drops 50 percent, bringing me back to my initial $20,000. The third year brings another 100 percent rate of returns, and again I have $40,000. However, year four brings another 50 percent decline, and I get back to my $20,000.

$20,000 INVESTMENT PLACED IN MUTUAL FUND FOR 4 YEARS		
YEAR	% RETURN	$RETURN
1	+100	$40,000
2	-50	$20,000
3	+100	$40,000
4	-50	$20,000
AVERAGE RETURN: +25% YIELD: 0%		

FIGURE 49: $20,000 in mutual fund performance outline over 4 years.
Notice "average return" versus "yield"

In this scenario, the mutual fund proudly announces a 25% average return, when, in fact, the actual yield is 0%. In the real world, the returns would be negative if we take into account all the variables such as inflation, taxes, fund expenses (the fund gets paid no matter what returns it brings), and lost opportunity costs.

Let's sum up the reality here. When investment money is lost in a bad year, the financial institutions continue to show supposed results of investment performance in the long run to prove that you'll make a positive return when all is said and done. Most are seriously lucky if they didn't lose any money. No matter how hard you work and how much you save, if you invest in the stock market, you'll probably be worse off than you were before you got in. Your money is paying for the salaries and bonuses of endless financial advisors, bankers, brokers, and many more individuals living off your losses. This means you probably can't retire in the lifestyle to which you would like to become accustomed – or even become financially stable!

Here's a typical scenario. A young couple decides to open a new brokerage account. They're excited about their new life together, and they were told to start a brokerage account. They visit their local brokerage office with $20,000 to invest. They meet with a stock broker (a sales person), and are told they can expect an average return of 10% per year. The couple scribbles furiously on a piece of paper as they discuss what they just heard. Example 1 shows what they calculated (and is, in fact, exactly what most people expect):

Example 1: Positive Returns

$20,000 INVESTMENT PLACED IN MUTUAL FUND FOR 4 YEARS		
YEAR	% RETURN	$RETURN
0	0	$20,000
1	10%	$22,000
2	10%	$24,200
3	10%	$26,620
4	10%	$29,282
AVERAGE RETURN: +10% ACTUAL YIELD: $9,282		

FIGURE 50: $20,000 in mutual fund performance with positive returns

Examples 2 and 3 will show you what they aren't told. Both of these generate an average return of 10% per year as well, although the couple really lost money with Example 3 and only broke even with Example 2!

In fact, it doesn't matter whether you gain, break even, or lose money, your broker tells you your average return is 10%. It happens because averages are not a good estimator of real profit. But you can determine the actual yield with the simple formula: Returns at the final year minus initial investment.

In Example 1, the annual yield was calculated at $9,282. The following charts show the performance of $20,000 invested over four years. All of them have an average return of 10% as well, but only one of them actually brings positive returns. This means that two out of three individuals get fooled into thinking they actually earned money investing in a mutual fund.

Example 2: Zero Returns

$20,000 INVESTMENT PLACED IN MUTUAL FUND FOR 4 YEARS		
YEAR	**% RETURN**	**$RETURN**
0	0	$20,000
1	58%	$31,620
2	-37%	$20,000
3	54%	$30,701
4	-35%	$20,000
AVERAGE RETURN: +10% **ACTUAL YIELD: $0**		

FIGURE 51: $20,000 in mutual fund performance with zero returns. Notice "average return" versus "yield"

Example 3: Negative Returns

$20,000 INVESTMENT PLACED IN MUTUAL FUND FOR 4 YEARS		
YEAR	**% RETURN**	**$RETURN**
0	0	$20,000
1	150%	$50,000
2	-20%	$40,000
3	-25%	$30,000
4	-65%	$10,500
AVERAGE RETURN: +10% **ACTUAL YIELD: -$9,500**		

FIGURE 52: $20,000 in mutual fund performance with negative returns

Another way to assess the real returns on stock market investments is using the Compound Annual Growth Rate (CAGR), the year-over-year growth rate of an investment over a specified period of time.

Open Your Eyes!

I'm not saying the stock market is bad. It has its place in the investing world. However, let's step back and consider the mantra my mentor keeps repeating: "Follow the money!"

Who's really making money from the stock market? Is it the individuals investing in this "poker" game, or is it the casino?

Who's the "casino" in this case? The financial institutions – the bankers – referred to as "shadow banks!" They make money no matter what happens to the market, whether it goes up or down, from various money management fees and other charges.

We're back to the bankers, still building wealth from our hard-earned money. Remember that bankers like to make money as safely as possible. The stock market provides another perfect vehicle for them. Consider the following questions.

- Do the bankers make fees every time a stock trade is done, whether the trade goes up or down? The answer is yes. And who takes the risk? Answer: The investor. Not the banker!

- Who makes money with mutual or hedge funds, managing consumers' money, whether the funds go up or down? Answer: The fund manager and the financial institution (shadow bank) they work for.

- Who takes the risk? Answer: The investors.

When investors invest in a hedge fund, they are typically charged a "2-20" – which means 2% of the assets under management (2% of the total money being managed) and 20% of the profit from the fund. So, for example, if a fund is $1M and that went up 8% to $1,080,000, the fund would charge as follows:

2% x $1,080,000 = $21,600
20% x $80,000 = $16,000
That equates to $21,600 + $16,000 = $37,600.

That might not seem like a lot. But let's look at it more closely. The fund made $80,000: $37,600 went to the financial institution, and you kept the remaining $42,400. So you invested $1M and received a 4.24% return.

Let's step back and consider this again.

DESCRIPTION	BANKER	INVESTOR
Risk *(Who is risking their money?)*	none	100%
Amount invested	$0	$1,000,000
Profit Sharing ($)	$37,600	$42,400
Profit Sharing (%)	47% of profit	53% of profit

FIGURE 53: Risk analysis of investment

In this example, the investor risks 100% of their money to get a little bit over half of the profit; the banker keeps the other half. And, in this situation, the fund actually makes money. Guess what happens if the fund *doesn't* make money? Yep, you guessed it! The investor loses their money, but the banker still makes their money by charging the 2% fees.

So, clearly, the shadow banks want us to invest in the stock market.

Having said that, one *can* use some elegant ways to invest wisely in the stock market. As with any advanced financing strategy, I strongly recommend that you get the right education before following *any* investing path.

To summarize, don't accept things at face value when it comes to the stock market and mutual funds.

Dr. Jazz adjusted his hat as we walked. "So, George, what's the fastest way to end up with a million dollars in the stock market?" he asked. Not waiting for an answer, he added: "Start with two million dollars."

I chuckled before asking, "Doctor, you talked about shadow banks, and you haven't mentioned them before. How many types of banks are there?" I asked curiously.

"Well, there are three types of banks. There's the corner bank, which is the neighborhood bank most people go to for their weekly deposits and withdrawals. This is the bank we all think about when we hear the word 'bank.' But there are two other types, as well. The first, a shadow bank, doesn't take direct deposits like your corner bank. Instead, they run hedge funds, money market funds, and structured investment vehicles. Many of the exotic investment vehicles you hear about in the news, such as mortgage-backed securities, happen within shadow banks. The third type is the central bank, which is the banks' bank. For example, the Federal Reserve of the United States is a central bank. They manage the creation of a nation's money supply and lend money to banks and other financial institutions. Many think of central banks as government agencies. They're not. They're controlled by the richest families in the world. They are powerful bankers."

That afternoon, as I drove back home, I realized I was tapping into some extremely potent information. Dr. Jazz had told me that some of the strategies I'm learning, or will eventually learn, from his wonderful manuscript are the same strategies that all three types of banks use. I was very excited and a little nervous. This was all new to me, and I had the feeling the doctor was leading up to something big.

The next morning, I decided to visit my mentor and talk to him about my experiences with Dr. Jazz.

Instead of talking, though, he gave me more homework.

CHAPTER SUMMARY

- The stock market is a minus-sum game.
- You're competing with the best of the best and with very fast computers.
- The stock market doesn't create wealth; it simply transfers wealth from one to another.
- The way returns are calculated in the stock market is not what you would expect and is not dependable.
- Financial institutions that are involved in the stock market shift risk to the people. These same financial institutions are known as shadow banks. They profit from our risks.
- If you're going to trade stocks, it's important to spend time educating yourself how to do it right.

Refer to the Resources page for a free bonus chapter with Dr. Jazz.

CHAPTER SIXTEEN

Build Your Team

MY MENTOR LEANED TOWARD ME AND SAID, "I HAVE GOOD NEWS AND I have bad news. Which one do you want to hear first?"

"Uh-oh! That doesn't sound good. Let's start with the bad news," I muttered.

"It's time to build your team, George. Dr. Jazz has shared some great information with you, but I want you to go ahead and focus on this, first," he said.

"What's so bad about that?" I asked curiously.

"Well," he laughed, "that's actually the good news, George. The bad news is, now you have to start filtering out the trash from the good. You have to figure out who's a good partner and who's out to hurt you. That's tough. That's the bad news. However, your team will also shape your life. I don't expect you to understand this for many years, yet," he said somberly, and I felt the depth his statement carried.

He bent his head and wrote down a few things on a piece of paper. It felt like a doctor's prescription as he placed it in my hand. The note included a simple, numbered list – the team members I needed to go out and find.

Here was my first assignment on the list.

1. Find the five most active real estate investors in the San Francisco Bay Area.

I firmly believed that if I focused on this strongly enough, the five would jump out at me. It's like when you decide to buy a specific car, you start noticing it everywhere.

Active Investor No. 1: Melvin

One day, three weeks after my meeting with my mentor, I was driving in downtown San Jose on Virginia Avenue to look at a property I was considering buying. As I drove by all the smaller, older homes, one house stood out. The house was fixed up, it had new paint, a beautiful and clean front yard with a new 'For Sale' sign staked in the middle, and a nice Porsche parked in front. It looked interesting. The front door was open, and I could tell the house was newly remodeled. It looked like an investor had bought it, remodeled it, and was about to sell it. I continued driving down the street.

My mind was racing, "What do I have to lose? What if I'm right, and this investor, this person, could be one of the five people I'm supposed to meet? I'll never know if I keep driving. I have nothing to lose," I thought.

I made a U-turn, headed back to the house, and parked my car behind the Porsche. I walked up the front path and then stepped through the front door....

"Hello. Anyone here?" I yelled as the sound echoed off the empty walls. I felt uncomfortable. What the heck was I doing in here?

"Yes, can I help you?" I heard a voice, and a man walked out from the kitchen with some electrical wires dangling from his hands. It looked like he was fixing some electrical problem.

He looked friendly enough and reached out to shake my hand. The man was a slender African-American, about 5'-9" tall, with a slight moustache and short hair. He wore shorts and a T-shirt.

I was nervous and started questioning myself. What am I doing here? Why am I bothering this guy? Finally, I found my voice.

"I was driving through the area and noticed this house. It looks great, a really excellent job. I assume you're the owner?" I said as I shook his hand.

"Yes, thank you. I'm selling it, also. Are you interested?" he chuckled.

"Well, actually, no, not really. I was so impressed by the work, though, I wanted to meet whoever did this. I do the same thing – I buy homes, fix them up, and sell them. And you've done such a good job, here. Can I take a look around?" I asked.

I was too unsure of myself to just blurt out that I was a private lender – since I had never done a loan with anyone! Yet this is exactly what my mentor had told me. He said I needed to start introducing myself as a private lender, and that would be awkward at first. He was right.

As we toured the house, we chatted. I didn't know it then, but before long we would become good friends. Melvin is methodical in his work and a very intelligent man, working as a successful investor, mainly on high-end homes. I also learned that he's a full-time fire fighter.

"What do *you* do?" he asked.

"Actually, I'm a private lender. I lend money to real estate investors," I said. I sighed inwardly and thought, "There, I did it." But I felt like a fake. I had never done a private loan, but my mentor's words kept echoing in my mind. "You're a private lender now!" He had promised that the time would soon come when I would not feel like a fish out of water. And it did....

Melvin would be the first of dozens of investors I would lend money to. I had my first investor...my first team member...DONE!

Active Investor No. 2: Gary

My phone was ringing, and I rushed from my bedroom to my office, 20 feet away, to pick it up.

A man named Gary introduced himself and said that two ladies had suggested he give me a call. (I had completed many private lending deals by this point, and my name was getting out there.) Apparently, he had asked them for the name of the most honest and ethical investor they knew, and they had referred him to me. I was both honored and embarrassed, but it *was* nice to know people saw that in me.

"How can I help you?" I asked Gary.

He had called for some advice. We chatted for more than 90 minutes, and I realized this guy was pretty smart. He was a "go-getter." I'm not easily impressed with the type, but this guy was different.

During the course of our conversation, I discovered that we had both been to the same university, UC Davis, at the same time, had the same major, been in the same classes, but didn't remember each other. Why? Because we had only occasionally shown up for class. I was working on an online gaming project to sell to CompuServe (an online company in the 1990s) at a time when no one else had online animated games, and Gary was doing his own thing.

I also discovered that this man had all the skills and knowledge of a successful marketer and real estate investor. Little did I know he would eventually become one of the most successful investors in the area as well as the founder of the country's largest direct-response-marketing company for real estate investors. As fate would have it, I would end up making some great money from a private loan with him months later, and years later we would end up business partners.

I had my second investor!

The process actually turned out to be easier than I had anticipated, and over the years I would find many other borrowers.

2. My second assignment: Find an attorney familiar with laws related to raising capital and capable of keeping me in compliance with those laws.

Where would I find this individual? I kept focusing on that. I interviewed many attorneys and learned a variety of things from them. I paid hundreds of dollars for their hourly rates, but it was some of the best money I had ever invested, money I would recoup many times over. Eventually, in 2005, I found my attorney.

As I turned the pages of a catalog of classes taught in the area, I came across a listing for a class about raising capital. The catalog description suggested that the class was what I was looking for, and the instructor – Jack – was the man I was told to look for. He had raised money through various funds for his real estate deals.

"*Oh, no!*" The class was starting in about an hour, I was in San Jose, and the class was being held in San Francisco, about an hour away. This was it; I had to go! I let my wife know where I was headed (She thought I was nuts for going!), and off I went.

I walked into the class 10 minutes late. As I walked through the door at the back of the classroom, up front I spotted a tall, slender guy (about 6'-6") in his early 30s. He was teaching the class of about 18 students.

"Can I help you?" he asked the man I assumed was Jack.

I'm not normally a joker, but it was one of those strange days, and I felt like cracking a joke.

"I'm here for the adult entertainment class, something about pole dancing and filming," I said with as straight a face as possible. I had no idea what I was saying, but I was going to see this through.

Everyone in the room turned to look at me, and the man I assumed correctly to be Jack blushed immediately and uncomfortably. With a bright red face, he stammered, "Uh…I'm sorry, but I think you have the wrong class."

"What class is this?" I asked.

"This class is about raising capital for investors," he said, feeling embarrassed for me.

"Yep. This is exactly the class I was looking for," I said with a mischievous smile. Everyone laughed, and I was relieved the joke went okay; otherwise, it could have gone downhill pretty quickly.

In spite of my rather disruptive wisecracking arrival, Jack would eventually agree to introduce me to raising capital. Over time, I learned a lot from Jack.

3. My third assignment: Find three hard-money brokers.

Hard-Money Broker No. 1: Jim

Walking down the stairs from my office towards the restroom, I bumped into a tall man with white hair. He was well dressed and seemed to be a friendly guy with an affable smile. I had seen him around the business building in which I leased an office.

"Hello. How are you?" I asked cordially as I passed, not expecting anything more than a simple reply. He responded kindly in turn, and we walked in and out of the restroom at the same time. We chuckled about that as we continued our conversation.

"By the way, my name is George. I'm in Suite 211," I said as I extended my hand (washed, by the way).

"Jim," he said as we shook hands.

"What do you do, Jim?" I asked.

He was a hard-money broker, with years of experience. Wow! What are the chances! We agreed to have lunch soon. Jim would, over time, teach me a lot about lending from the broker's perspective.

I had found my first hard-money broker!

Hard-Money Broker No. 2: Bob

I had searched online for another hard-money broker and found one named Bob, but I was hesitating, too nervous to call. What if I sounded like an idiot? Who am I to talk to these people?

Once again I asked myself, "What do I have to lose?" So I picked up the phone and called Bob. We discussed what he does as a broker and eventually met for lunch.

Bob was an older, down-to-earth, very kind man. He had been an extremely successful businessman and real estate investor (clearly intelligent) in his younger years, and we clicked immediately. He was retired and enjoyed dabbling in private money, and before long we were meeting regularly – once a quarter or so – at a *Chili's* restaurant in Cupertino. It was always a joy to talk to this man with so much experience, and little did I realize that Bob would teach me so much about private money lending as well. I had my second hard-money broker! In fact, before long I had assembled my team of hard-money brokers, and they were ready to go.

4. My fourth assignment: Find an escrow service.

I had closed real estate deals with several title companies, and so I decided to talk to them about my lending plans and about some of the creative things I had learned.

For instance, I had learned that, unfortunately, very few people wanted to handle anything outside the norm. Their norm was simple purchase and refinance transactions.

But I had in mind transactions that were slightly different, and I was frustrated that no one was even willing to listen. Escrow-service companies hire staff to handle their "normal" transactions; I needed to connect directly with the branch managers, the ones with 10 to 20 years of experience. They would understand what I was trying to do.

And so I ended up finding a lady named Mary Jane to handle some of my transactions. MJ was an amazing woman with the friendliest of faces; she always had a smile. I knew I could depend on her for guidance and her willingness to handle complicated escrows. Together, we would learn a lot. I had my escrow person in place!

5. My fifth assignment: Find the best coach on the planet.

My fifth assignment was the toughest. I found that there were many coaches. In fact, it seemed that everyone called themselves a coach. I wasn't even sure what a coach was supposed to be, or do, for that matter. I just knew that many of the most successful individuals had coaches. Tiger Woods had a coach, Michael Jordan had a coach, and so did many others.

I recall my mentor saying, "A coach sees the potential in you that you don't yet see in yourself."

I tried working with many coaches, but none really worked out. They just didn't seem to click. My mentor always reminded me that a coach "would push me to the limits, where I would come close to hating them, but that I would come through a much-more-successful person. A coach is not your friend. A coach will change your life. Coaches will push you more than anyone else will because they believe in you more than you believe in yourself." I wanted that.

Eventually, several years later, I would find that person. He was a well-known and respected man named Willie Hooks. But when I first met him, it wasn't obvious he would be the man.

I walked into a meeting on the 9th floor of a nice building in Walnut Creek a few minutes late. Except for one gentleman with a serious look on his face, I knew everyone there, including Gary (my UC Davis class-mate). We all exchanged pleasantries, and I was introduced to Willie Hooks as we all sat down.

After much discussion about some of the things we were working on, I noticed this fellow was a man of few words. He seemed to be observing and listening. He didn't say much, but the little he said seemed to carry a lot of wisdom.

After several such meetings, I could see that this very wise man had what it took to succeed. And he knew how to help others succeed as well. He had made more millionaires than any other person I had known, and he would eventually become my coach!

I had gone through a lot of coaches, but this was the one. Now I was ready.

I had built a team that most people would envy. During the time I was building my team, I had begun private lending. At last it was time to really rock and roll!

"I cannot stress enough the importance of having the right partners in your life. A wrong partner can devastate you, while the right partner can take you to new heights," continued my mentor. "Look at the times where just one principal affected the lives of everyone in the firm. There are so many stories where one of these individuals stole or embezzled money, made foolish decisions, or behaved irresponsibly, negatively affecting the reputation and integrity of every individual in the company. Make sure you don't underestimate the significance of what I'm telling you," he said sternly.

He continued, and I listened, believing that nothing like this would ever happen to me. Little did I know that, many years later, the same horrible thing would happen to me. It would be a hard and painful lesson.

My mentor's advice about building a team changed my life. I made my share of bad choices along the way, but I also made some very good choices. Through dedication and searching, I learned what my mentor's intention was. Building a team is a journey. It's a part of your wealth life. Individuals we meet during childhood and beyond, throughout our life — the good ones and the bad — leave their marks on us. They all help to make us who we are today.

With this team, I would go on to build my wealth. Over the years the team transformed. Some ended up being friends, some I learned a lot from, others would make me money, while others would guide me. Along the way they all contributed to my eventual success.

To them, I say this: Thank you for being part of my life and success. I'm happy and grateful to call you friends. You have shaped my life.

I wondered what Dr. Jazz would think of my thoughts.

CHAPTER SUMMARY

- Find five, active real estate investors in the area.
- Find an expert in raising capital and have them teach you how to do it.
- Find three hard-money brokers.
- Find an escrow company.
- Find a great coach.
- Finally, make sure to get the right training.

Refer to the Resources page for a free bonus chapter with Dr. Jazz.

CHAPTER SEVENTEEN

Leaving A Legacy

Dr. Jazz slowly opened the manuscript to a page with a diagram that looked like a flowchart or family tree. The title at the very top of the page said, "Leaving a Legacy," and was subtitled, "Passing It to the Next Generation."

"George, I want you to think about something. Did you know that the wealth most people work hard to accumulate — once it's passed on to their children — is gone within two generations?

"Yet, there are certain families that have had ancestral wealth for many generations," he continued. "There are several reasons for that, but it's important you realize that you have to address that issue early on," he said.

I was just interested in putting these concepts to use. I wasn't even thinking about my grandchildren yet; my oldest child was barely a teenager at the time! But I decided to keep listening. After all, this man was full of wisdom.

"And with banking, it's easier than you think to pass these lessons to the next generation.

"It's believed that the Rothschilds, the greatest banking dynasty the world has ever known, meet once a year, continuing to pass their knowledge and experience onto the next generation. They educate the younger ones, never

giving them money, always lending it to them, helping to ensure that their legacy continues," said the doctor.

At first this made no sense to me until I saw it all explained in the manuscript. He smiled at me and pointed to the open page.

"Have patience and it will all make more sense. I followed the same principles. For example, when my children began their schooling, I lent them the money, and they had to pay it back just as they would any other student loan. At first, my wife was mad at me ... "

I couldn't believe what I was hearing and interrupted him, "Doctor, I would be, too! They're your *kids, and I think you should consider* giving *them the money for their schooling,* not *lending it to them. Where's the love?" I asked.*

He paused for a few moments and just stared at me. The silence was deafening!

Then he smiled, and I felt better. He continued, "George, that's the consumer thinking. I want you to see the banker's side. Is that okay with you?" he asked me sarcastically.

"So, I'll repeat myself," he chided and then continued. "When my children began their schooling, I lent them the money, using my banking system. They had to pay it back, just as they would any other loan. At first, my wife was mad at me, but when I explained it to her, she understood. Here's what I said to her.

"Whose money is it in the long run? It's theirs, my children's. After I'm gone, all of that money is theirs. But by lending it to them, I'm passing on the lessons of being the lender. They're learning that this money should always be lent and never taken out. If this lesson is taught early to the young, it becomes part of their reality. So they, too, will pass these lessons to the next generation, while their money continues to grow, once again ready to be passed to future generations.

"Consumers have been conditioned to believe that money in a piggy bank must be saved and then used to buy something. In reality, money in a piggy bank must always be borrowed and paid back with interest. That's how lessons are learned and wealth accumulated for future generations. By lending

them money for the big purchases, like cars, schooling, and the like, we're teaching real-life lessons they'll never forget.

"This is the best gift you can give your children. That's why I believe the Rothschilds are still so dominant," Dr. Jazz concluded.

The more he spoke, the more I wished I had never opened my mouth. I was wrong yet again, and I came to the realization that many times we say things simply to justify our position instead of listening and being open to new ideas.

"What else would one lend money to their children for?" I asked. You talked a little about schooling and cars. What else?" I was pretty sure I understood, but I wanted to be sure.

"Well, most people buy a car every five years. If your children start at the age of 20, following that pattern they will have purchased nine cars by the time they're 65. Those purchases, by themselves, if handled correctly with a banking system, could produce results in the high six to low seven figures! Imagine, being able to do that for your three kids!

"Next, consider their schooling. Same methods, similar results. Furthermore, they'll probably have to rent living quarters at some point. You can lend them the rent money, and if they rent for seven years, paying $1,000 a month...well, that will be a very big number. Of course, they'll probably want furniture loans and loans for their pricey electronic toys and other expensive things that people buy. And one day, when they start their business, they'll need loans for equipment and to cover other expenses. These alone could put seven figures into your banking system that you can pass along to them." At this point he stopped and looked at me keenly.

My mouth dropped! Why didn't my father know about this and lend me the money for my school, I thought.

I was finally beginning to see things from the banker's perspective and understand why they think so differently from consumers and producers. And more important, I understood how they make money, keep it, and pass it on to the next generation.

Dr. Jazz chuckled and patted me gently on the back as he went on to explain how he uses certain entities to manage his wealth for tax benefits, helping his children and charities capture the wealth with as little tax burdens as possible.

That evening I shared this information with my wife and found myself understanding it more and more. Banking is much more than making money. It's a major shift in mindset. Bankers just think differently.

It's about making money in a safer position, using finance strategies to increase yields (return), and simply thinking differently. It's about adopting the mindset and the rules of the banker. I recognized that becoming the banker wouldn't be easy, but I knew that the persistent ones are the ones earning their stripes.

The most important thing Dr. Jazz had said to me was this: "Most people spend their lives searching for a path to follow. Many find a path too late, and many others simply never find a path. Now that you know the path, assuming you want to be the lender, you're way ahead of most people. Dedicate your life to following that path and ultimately mastering that skill, for most people are simply lost and still searching. The information I have shared with you, George, has allowed you to gain a lifetime of lessons. Commit to it, recognize there will be challenges along the way, accept them, and move forward. Making that firm decision of being the lender and committing to it is 50% of the challenge. Go out and prosper."

Dr. Jazz had convinced me that I wanted to be a private lender. In fact, later that evening, I got a call about some of the rentals properties I had purchased years ago in another state. One property had been vandalized and another needed a new roof. That news made me realize that I really wanted to be a private lender!

Early the next morning my cell phone rang, cruelly awakening me.

It was my mentor. "George, I'm sorry for calling so early and waking you, but I have some bad news."

He had never called me this early before.

"Dr. Jazz has passed away. He went to bed last night and never woke up. This is terrible news, just horrible. He was such a great man," sobbed my mentor.

I fought the tears in my eyes as I sank slowly back onto the bed.

CHAPTER SUMMARY

- Consider how financially important it is that you teach your children to think like bankers. Begin by *lending* them money that will ultimately belong to them. You will be leaving them with money and a lifetime of lessons that they too can pass along.

Refer to the Resources page for a free
bonus chapter with Dr. Jazz.

CHAPTER EIGHTEEN

The Secret Society

I PULLED ON THE HEAVY DOOR AND WAS NOT SURPRISED TO FIND A ROOM full of people. I joined them, somberly mourning the loss of Dr. Jazz. This special man had touched the lives of so many people, and I was, again, grateful for the precious time I had been given with him.

I quickly relived the past few months in my mind as uneasy thoughts assailed me. Thank goodness my mentor had brought Dr. Jazz into my life. Thank goodness my mentor thought I was worthy of the meeting. I felt such gratitude that I could barely breathe. And I was nervous. My mentor had sounded so cryptic on the phone about today that I was filled with apprehension.

But I was heartened by the voices of his family and the laughter of his grandchildren celebrating Dr. Jazz's life, and I turned to see France's tear-stained face. We hugged without speaking and chatted softly with the children.

I stood as I recognized my mentor approaching, his visage somber.

"George," he said quietly, "Dr. Jazz would be pleased that you came. I'm glad you're here, and as I told you, I have a surprise for you. Come with me; I want to introduce you to some special people."

We walked through a back door, down a narrow hallway, and entered a back room, inviting and comfortably lit. A private celebration of sorts was happening; a couple dozen or so people were in the room.

"My friends," my mentor began, "this is Dr. Jazz's last student, George." They greeted me warmly, welcoming me, to what *I had not yet figured out.*

"You remember," he said to me, "that Dr. Jazz's special manuscript was only one of seven copies given to him by Herbert." He spread his arms and pointed around the room. "All these people are here because they, too, were students of Dr. Jazz's and Herbert's. They, too, owe their success to the teachings in that special manuscript." I glanced at the others in the room with a new perspective.

He guided me to a table in the center of the room, and we were joined by six others as we sat. The rest of the guests quietly surrounded us.

The room had become hushed, the mood somber. "I asked you to join us, George, at the special request of Dr. Jazz. He was very impressed with you, as I knew he would be," my mentor said proudly. "He talked to many of us here about you, as well, and arranged for you to have this before his death. He asked that we present it to you, along with a very special invitation." As my mentor spoke, the tall, elegant woman to my left gingerly placed the familiar manuscript in front of me.

"This manuscript, and all its secrets, are now yours," my mentor continued, and I was unsure of what to say.

I sat there for a moment in the quiet, running my hands over the weathered leather, taking in the scent of the manuscript, remembering the lessons with Dr. Jazz. The tears were too close. I noticed a weathered page sticking out of the manuscript; it had never been there before. I hoped no one had torn any pages from my new property and was determined to find out as soon as possible. "I'm honored," I began, "and I'll make sure..."

"You can be honored all you want," my mentor smiled, "but this gift comes with great responsibilities, with certain stipulations." I noticed the others nodding in agreement, and he grew serious once again. "I know Dr. Jazz spoke to you briefly about the responsibilities that accompany this gift. I also know that he was taken from us before he had time to tell you more.

"You see, George, Herbert wanted to be sure that these secrets reached as many people as possible and that they would be able to initiate real change, change that would bring great success to many. And so he endowed great accountability with those that learned the manuscript's secrets.

"Years ago, Dr. Jazz, at the request of his mentor, was asked to accept a great responsibility. He was asked to create and coordinate an association of individuals, all bequeathed with the knowledge found in the manuscripts – to be clear, a 'Secret Society.' All of us in this room, upon receipt of the manuscript, were invited into the society and accepted the doctrines and responsibilities that come with it," my mentor continued.

"As part of this society, this inner circle, we meet twice or more a year to touch base, exchange lessons learned, share stories, meet new private lenders, share opportunities, and celebrate each other's successes. We call these days "Platinum Days," and many of us fly from around the country – the world really – to be together. Some of us are still apprentices, and others become mentors and help the newer people. This is about a community that aims to be not just the most advanced private lenders in the world, but more important, to be a community that helps each other succeed," my mentor concluded.

I could feel the sense of passion and community in that room. I felt so privileged to be amongst these people. It felt genuine and real.

The gentleman across the table spoke. "When I met Herbert, I was only 16, homeless, and living in the alley behind the restaurant where Herbert liked to have his afternoon tea." I remembered meeting Mr. Macy minutes before and was impressed by his quiet dignity and intelligent eyes.

"I, too, have one of Herbert's manuscripts, and he made me promise that I would share this knowledge with at least seven others. Several of them are here with us tonight, and each one of them has committed to sharing their knowledge with seven others."

"I, too, am an apprentice," the graceful woman to my left said. Her British accent was charming, made more so by the kindness in her smile. "I received mine from my mentor, who received it many years ago. And I, too, promised to share my awareness with at least seven others, and each of those promised to share with seven more. You understand? We learn. We share."

She waved to a group of people behind my mentor, and they laughed in unison as they waved back. The others around the table and throughout the room all began to nod and speak softly in consensus.

My mentor took my arm, and began to walk me around the room, introducing me one by one to these amazing individuals from all walks of life, men and women with stories of their own to tell. And as we journeyed around the room, I began to recognize the possibilities my mentor and Dr. Jazz had been teaching me about were here, all around me. Once again, I thanked my lucky stars for the tutelage, guidance, and patience my mentor and Dr. Jazz had given me. I wasn't sure what I had done to be so lucky, but I was beginning to understand why I had been feeling nervous when I got here.

I met a gentleman who had been a penniless drifter when he met Herbert. He told me of the many things he had been taught and how he had used that knowledge to build one of the largest chains of banks on the East Coast. "The possibilities are endless," he said. "You were lucky, my friend, to have been guided by Dr. Jazz as much as you were... but you're just getting started! There is so much more to know! Allow us all to help you learn more." I was fascinated by his story, how he had literally stumbled into Herbert, resulting in an ugly mess of hot dogs, relish, and mustard.

He introduced me to his three daughters, now running their banking dynasty. They teased me with remarkable stories of lending, and I laughed as they told me about their own sons and daughters, some in the business and some not, but all of whom were continuing the family tradition of sharing this amazing knowledge.

A small, rotund gentleman excitedly greeted my mentor and introduced himself. "George, I wanted to talk to you about Dr. Jazz," he said. "He called me several weeks ago about you, but I was out of the country and unable to meet with him. By the time I got home, well ...." He stopped and shook his head. "I live in Palo Alto and have some interesting connections that the Doctor wanted me to explore with you. I would be honored if you would care to join me for lunch next week, and we can talk more about how I can help you," and he handed me his card. "We can both share stories about Dr. Jazz and his fondness for walks," he laughed.

We chuckled and my mentor said, "Ah, he's being modest. Joel is the CEO of a national restaurant franchise chain, as well as on the board of several other public companies." I was surprised. Joel looked so young, only a few years older than myself.

"I was the manager of a fast food restaurant in Walnut Creek when I met Dr. Jazz," Joel said. He looked off to his right, remembering another time, and grinned. "It was so funny. He bought one of those children's meals, you know, for one of his granddaughters, and the toy was the wrong one. She wanted one of the other toys used in the promotion, and he was trying to explain it all to me, and all the while his granddaughter was having hysterics, crying and screaming about that darned toy.... He was so patient, so loving and kind to her, and that impressed me. Most parents would not have been so nice. We became instant allies and, later, good friends. I'll miss those walks."

As we moved around the room, I took a short break to step out and find a quiet corner to quell my curiosity. I had been worrying about that page I had seen sticking out of the manuscript and reached for it.

"My dear George," the Doctor had written across the top. "I have been honored to know you and am a better man because of it," he continued. I was surprised and touched to my core. "I have thoroughly enjoyed your endless questions and strategizing with you and all the lessons we shared together. But please know, my friend, that, unfortunately, we only had a short time to share.

"Your goals will guide your actions, and your actions will or will not guarantee your success. Please keep your word to yourself and to your goals. You are now part of a powerful society composed of some of the most remarkable people in the world. Learn from them. Grow with them...."

There was more, but I couldn't continue. I made my way to the restrooms to wash my face before I rejoined the others.

As I continued around the room, I instantly recognized from countless media interviews a successful entrepreneur and philanthropist. "Yes," he said in response to my comments and questions, "Dr. Jazz was an amazing man. Most people have no idea how much he gave back to the community, to many communities. George, we all have very big shoes to fill." I remembered the recent scene in the Doctor's office, and he continued, "That banking system stuff is incredible, isn't it, George? That's how I get to spend so much time with my favorite projects, you know. Love to talk to you more about that, if you want. The Doctor showed me some cool strategies I can share with you."

Next, my mentor introduced me to an elderly woman in a blue sequined dress. "George, Mrs. Reilly used to work for Joel at one of his restaurants. She was his best waitress, and now she has her own restaurants — and three generations of Reilly's she's teaching!" he boasted.

"And working on the fourth, now," she giggled with delight. "I hear through the grapevine that you have an inquisitive nature, my boy," she said. "I hope you never lose that. Here, please sit with me a minute while I steal you away from your mentor." She laughed and patted my hand, fiercely clutching the manuscript.

"There are so many fascinating and wonderful things in that book you're holding onto for dear life, George, and I want you to know that every single one of us here in this room is still learning its brilliance. And as we learn, we share. That, my new friend, is one of the very cool bennies, as my granddaughter likes to say, that comes with being a member of our secret society. You have much to learn, and that wondering mind of yours will be seeking answers. Ask for them from all of us here. Keep wondering, George. Keep asking questions. And have fun along the way!"

I wanted to ask her more, but my mentor interrupted us. "George, I know you have many questions, but there's someone special I want you to meet." He again took my arm, and we walked slowly toward a shadowed figure in a dimmed corner of the room.

"I'm so proud of you, George. And so was Dr. Jazz. You're asking all the right questions. And now, I'd like you to meet someone that has more of the right answers, someone who also was mentored by Dr. Jazz. The professor is one of the more amazing individuals you'll meet here. He's taken this powerful knowledge, and…well, I'll let him tell you more.

My body felt numb from racing through so many emotions this evening, and I wasn't sure I could handle more surprises, but my mentor was bursting with excitement.

His energy was rubbing off on me, and we stopped in front of the very, intriguing shadow in the corner. The gentleman was hunched over the table, writing furiously on scraps of paper. He barely glanced at me as we were introduced, and I wondered why my mentor was so excited.

But the information he would share with me over the coming months could potentially change the lives of millions of people....

RESOURCES

Additional Information

For more details, visit *www.TheBankersCodeBook.com*

Free Bonus Chapter

If you would like to have a free, bonus chapter with continuing conversations and information Dr. Jazz shared with the author, just visit *www.TheBankersCodeBook.com*.

Qualified Retirement Plan

A QRP is a retirement account that allows an investor and/or private lender to save approximately ten times the amount they could save in an IRA. The investor/private lender gets checkbook control, so there is no begging the custodian for their own funds. Furthermore, the investor can borrow up to $50,000 out of the account for personal use.

For additional information, visit *www.TheBankersCodeBook.com*

Grab *The Wealthy Code* Best Selling Book Today!

For additional information, visit *www.TheWealthyCodeBook.com*

Contact Information

Company: WealthClasses LLC
Toll-free phone: (888) 888-3612
Web: *www.WealthClasses.com*
E-mail: *TheBankersCodeBook@wealthclasses.com*

INDEX